I got to spend some time with Bill early on in my faith journey, and he was instrumental in moving me a little closer to Jesus. We may seem to be unlikely friends—after all, our ministry styles and hairdos are a little different . . . but I am forever grateful for the lives that have come to know Jesus through the life and ministry of Bill Bright.

SHANE CLAIBORNE
Author, Activist and Recovering Sinner
www.thesimpleway.org

If you're longing for a deeper Christian experience, for holiness rather than hype, here is an opportunity to sit at the feet of an unassuming and joyful saint. Dr Bill Bright was one of the twentieth century's great Christian leaders, and yet he considered himself nothing more than a slave. I would encourage anyone who wants to change the world for Jesus to read this book slowly. Share it with others. Pray through its many challenges. And then begin to rewrite it daily as the legacy of your own life as well.

PETE GREIG
24-7 Prayer, Alpha International
Author of *Red Moon Rising* and *God on Mute*

Bill was truly a world-changer who had one of the greatest impacts for the gospel in the twentieth century. *My Life is Not My Own* captures his heart and vision and will challenge us all to learn from his example.

SEAN McDOWELL
Educator, Speaker and Co-author of *Evidence for the Resurrection*

Bill Bright has had an impact on the lives of thousands of people through his ministry and his life. In *My Life Is Not My Own*, we discover a big reason for this impact and get clear insight into what motivated Bill Bright as he discusses the importance of genuine surrender to Jesus Christ. Each chapter will both challenge you and inspire you to trust God at a deeper level. This is an important book for all believers.

PHILIP WAGNER

Lead Pastor, Oasis Church, Los Angeles, CA
Co-Author, *God Chicks and the Men They Love*
Founder of Generosity Water (generositywater.com)

BILL BRIGHT

FOUNDER, CAMPUS CRUSADE FOR CHRIST

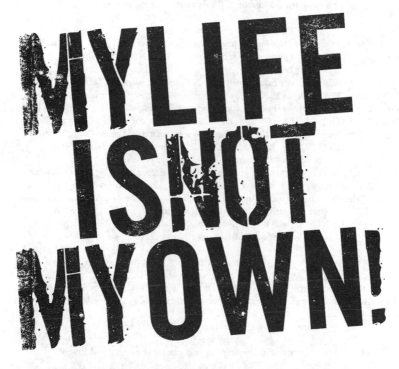

MY LIFE IS NOT MY OWN!

FOLLOWING GOD NO MATTER THE COST

Regal

From Gospel Light
Ventura, California, U.S.A.

Published by Regal
From Gospel Light
Ventura, California, U.S.A.
www.regalbooks.com
Printed in the U.S.A.

Library of Congress Cataloging-in-Publication Data
Bright, Bill.
My life is not my own : following God no matter the cost / Bill Bright.
p. cm.
ISBN 978-0-8307-5499-1 (hard cover)
1. Obedience—Religious aspects—Christianity. I. Title.
BV4647.O2B75 2010
241'.4—dc22
2010013046

1 2 3 4 5 6 7 8 9 10 11 12 13 14 15 / 20 19 18 17 16 15 14 13 12 11 10

Rights for publishing this book outside the U.S.A. or in non-English languages are
administered by Gospel Light Worldwide, an international not-for-profit ministry.
For additional information, please visit www.glww.org, email info@glww.org, or write
to Gospel Light Worldwide, 1957 Eastman Avenue, Ventura, CA 93003, U.S.A.

To order copies of this book and other Regal products in bulk quantities,
please contact us at 1-800-446-7735.

*To my beloved Vonette, who joined me
in making the life-changing decision
to become a "slave of Jesus."*

Dr. Bill Bright

*To our sons, Zac and Brad,
who lived with our decision
and continue the legacy of serving Jesus.*

Vonette Bright

CONTENTS

A FAMILY OF SERVANTS

Zac Bright

This book is about the paradox of belonging to Jesus Christ: that the way up is down, that there is no Crown without a Cross, that God makes a way where there is no way, that one must become like a child to enter the kingdom of God, that the greatest in the kingdom of God is the servant of all, that God provides for our needs when we don't strive to meet them, that God brings life out of death, and that obedience to Jesus is true freedom. In short, "the truth will make you free" (John 8:32, *NRSV*), and "if the Son makes you free, you will be free indeed" (John 8:36, *NRSV*).

My father was suffused with joy in knowing and serving Jesus. Lightness, hilarity and laughter characterized his experience. He was delighted that Jesus makes even the challenging aspects of life, like obedience and discipline, to serve God's glory and our happiness. One way that my father would try to provoke this insight was to observe impishly, "I am just a slave of Jesus Christ." This should always be said with élan and panache!

My parents marked this belonging to Jesus early in their life together by signing a contract with Jesus: He would meet all their needs and they would turn over all areas of their lives to His use. Of course this meant trusting God not only for their own needs but also for the needs of their children. My father would often say things like "you can't out-give God" and "God will not be a debtor to anyone." He would say that though we never had a lot of money, God had blessed us with houses, vacations, travel, adventures and education in abundance. When needs arose, we would pray, and God always took care of us. Even small details were brought to God in prayer. I can't count how many times car or house keys were misplaced and my father would say, "Let's pray about it" and immediately the keys would be found.

All of us must serve and worship someone or something: the living God or an idol. What I learned at an early age in my family is that only Jesus truly satisfies. Many people live many frustrating years before they learn this lesson. Others, sadly, never learn. Whether it's possessions, fame, reputation, nation, ideology, family or pleasure, no idol can take the weight of my life and happiness. Only Jesus can take the weight of my life. Blessed are those who learn to rejoice in necessity: "I have been bought with a price; I am not my own. I am a slave of Jesus Christ, and I am so stoked about it!"

Rev. Zachary D. Bright
Divine Savior Presbyterian Church

SERVING IS A LIFESTYLE
Brad Bright

It was an "aha" moment when I finally began to grasp what made my dad tick.

One day, shortly after I graduated from college, a young reporter from a Christian magazine came to interview my dad. "Dr. Bright," he said, "could you share a problem you face that the average Joe Christian can relate to?"

"I don't have any problems," my dad replied with quiet confidence. The reporter responded, "Dr. Bright, don't over-spiritualize. We all have problems." Suppressing his frustration, the reporter repeated the question several different ways, always receiving the same response.

Finally, my dad looked him directly in the eye and said, "Young man, you need to understand something. I am a slave of Jesus. It is not the slave's responsibility to be successful, but simply to do what the Master asks. When you understand this, you will realize you don't have problems. All that's left are opportunities to see the Master work."

At that moment, it hit me: My dad actually believed with every fiber of his being what he had just said. That experience created a seismic paradigm shift in my thinking that eventually sunk in and changed my life. The true genius of Bill Bright was his view of God.

The reporter didn't get what he wanted that day, but sitting in the background, I got what *I* needed. For years I had watched my dad respond to challenging circumstances and gut-wrenching decisions with a peace and confidence that defied reason. I admired, respected and loved my dad, but I knew I could never be like him . . . until that day. It's not that I wanted to "be" Bill Bright; we're two very different men. But I *can* daily become a slave of Jesus just like he did. I can live life problem-free, full of opportunities to see God work.

Today, I have learned to ask two questions whenever a "problem" comes along: First, "Am I going to *choose* to believe this is a problem, or an opportunity to see God work?" If I am still struggling to believe that it is truly an "opportunity," then I ask myself this follow-up question: "What attribute of God am I struggling to believe is true in this situation?"

I haven't arrived yet, but the journey begun that day has revolutionized my life. Thanks, Dad, for choosing to be a slave of Jesus and modeling for me what it looks like to have a huge view of our magnificent God!

Brad Bright
President and CEO, Bright Media
National Director, DISCOVER GOD

LEADERSHIP IS PASSED ON

Steve Douglass

There is a tremendous need for Christians to reflect Christlike character to our hurting world. My heart has been burdened for some time with questions about the choices we make every day. Will we be able to fulfill all that God has called us to do? My burden is not related to an organizational strategy, but more specifically to our individual relationships with God.

In John 15:5, Jesus said, "Yes, I am the vine; you are the branches. Those who remain in me, and I in them, will produce much fruit. For apart from me you can do nothing." So there is our choice: nothing or everything. It all hinges on whether we depend on God. Are we completely dependent on God in our thoughts and actions?

As I serve in my position today with Campus Crusade for Christ, I realize that many who have gone before me made the choice to totally depend on God. We need their example to encourage us to live every day making the choice to give ourselves in total surrender to the will of God.

I worked closely with Bill Bright for well over 30 years before God called him home. By God's grace he possessed many extraordinary qualities. One of them was his willingness to totally set aside his agenda to live out God's agenda. He would often say that he had no "rights" because he was bought with the price of Christ's death on the cross.

Most Christians understand the concept of the price Christ paid for our salvation. But very few people make the choice to surrender to Christ as Lord of their lives. Bill not only understood that truth, but he also lived it out. He chose not to own a car or a house. He gave away his pension to sponsor a training center in Moscow. He believed he should have as little interest in the things of this world as a dead man would. He realized that he had died to the world and had become subject to God.

So when it came time for him to select what inscription would be put on his gravestone, he and Vonette chose: *A Slave of Jesus by Choice*.

Here was a man who showed he was willing to endure the raised eyebrows and verbal scorn of others to openly live his life as a slave of Jesus Christ—cheerfully doing whatever He told him to do.

Bill's life serves as an example to us all of what can be accomplished when a person chooses to totally humble himself before God.

Steve Douglass
President, Campus Crusade for Christ International

A SHARED MINISTRY

Vonette Bright

As Bill and I planned our wedding, we searched for just the right song to be sung. We agreed on "O Jesus, I Have Promised," which features lyrics by John E. Bode (1816–1874) that very well declared our hearts' commitment. We asked that it be sung in the plural for us as a couple:

O Jesus we have promised to serve Thee to the end; Be Thou forever near us, our Master and our Friend. We shall not fear the battle if Thou art by our side, nor wander from the pathway if Thou wilt be our guide.

O Jesus let us hear Thee speaking in accents clear and still, above the storms of passion, the murmurs of self-will. O speak to reassure us to hasten or control; O speak and make us listen, Thou guardian of our souls.

O Jesus, Thou hast promised to all who follow Thee, that where Thou art in glory, there shall thy servants be. And, Jesus, we have promised to serve Thee to the end; O give us grace to follow, our Master and our Friend.

Little did we know that two years and a few months later, the word "Master" would have an even deeper meaning to us. We chose to be slaves to our Master and our Friend. Bill led in the decision, and I wanted to follow him as my husband, in full partnership. It was a mutual surrender and submission unlike anything we had ever considered before.

Let me point out, I have never felt like a slave in the way the word is commonly understood. I have never been forced into doing something that I did not choose to do. Of course, it has grieved my heart to see across the world so many women who are treated not only as coerced human slaves, but are even viewed as subhuman by the males of their cultures. I have never had feelings of being a second-class person in any way. When I received the Lord Jesus into my heart and life, I felt all the more free as I found my identity in Him. Then, I was blessed to experience the privilege of freely *choosing* to submit myself utterly and completely to Jesus Christ, in the same way as did Mary, the mother of Jesus.

When presented with the opportunity to accept God's wondrous plan for her life, she responded, "My soul exalts the Lord, and my Spirit has rejoiced in God my Savior. For He has had regard for the humble estate of His bondslave" (Luke 1:46-48, NASB). Literally, the Bible authors note, "i.e. a female slave."

There was no pressure on me when Bill and I decided together that fateful Sunday afternoon to make our special and complete surrender to Jesus. We gave up everything we had or would ever have. We surrendered everything we were and ever would be. This was not a burdensome, reluctant submission, and we did not get up from our knees with a sense of great obligation. In fact, just the opposite happened. There was a great sense of relief and release. We surrendered all that we had been striving so hard to achieve in our own strength. My goals were not unusual—a home nice enough to receive the president of the United States and modest enough that a homeless person would feel comfortable; children to bless and to be blessed by; and opportunities to travel, serve and speak.

But after we signed our contracts to be slaves of Jesus, these goals were secondary to keeping Jesus as our first love, the Lord and Master of our lives; and if the goals were to come to pass, it would be by His doing, by His Spirit, by His power. In that moment, we laid down everything that represented us. And when we made the commitment of our hearts and lives, we were free at last to serve Christ unhindered by worldly and selfish distractions. God proceeded through the years to give us everything we previously had dreamed and more. We learned that you cannot outgive God. He has provided exceedingly abundantly above what we could ask or think.

Perhaps that is why I was not overwhelmed or even surprised when Bill enthusiastically greeted me the next morning after he had been up all night studying with a friend for a Hebrew exam. He announced that God had given him a vision for the creation of a movement to help reach the entire world with the gospel of Jesus Christ. The name Campus Crusade for Christ International was suggested to us by Dr. Wilbur Smith, esteemed professor of the New Testament. God is not only good, but He is also great and greatly to be praised; He is trustworthy. You can give Him your "everything" and He will make it "something special" for eternity.

So it is a great honor and joy for me to offer this Preface to a very special book by a very special man. Bill Bright was my friend, lover and partner; my minister and my mentor; father to our sons, grandfather to our grandchildren and an enthusiastic ambassador of the Lord we serve. For 54 years, 6 months and 20 days of marriage he made me feel special. I still stand in awe at what God can do with a couple from Oklahoma who is willing to give Him all and let Him make them the kind of people He wants them to be.

Apart from our salvation, our choice to become slaves of Jesus was the best decision we ever made, and I commend it to you with all my heart.

Bill and I had many opportunities to make choices that would impact not only our lives but also the lives of our children, our families and our staff. Bill has captured some key thoughts for every believer, and we have included those for you as "choice points." You can fulfill God's purpose for your life as you choose to surrender to Him.

I have spent many hours reading and rereading this manuscript. On July 19, 2003, my dear Bill left this world. My reflections on our life together and the ministry we so enjoyed bring me great comfort.

Bill spent many hours preparing this manuscript, because he felt so strongly that the message had to be properly communicated and accurately represent the power of our awesome God.

Many Campus Crusade for Christ staff had asked him questions about what it meant to be a slave for Christ. He could never speak about the founding of Campus Crusade for Christ without weeping. It was a very sacred moment in his life. When he learned he had a terminal illness, he had 89 projects we wanted to complete.

Bill wanted us to write this book together. Frankly, in a sense, I didn't feel worthy. He was so quick to trust God. If the Bible said something, he believed it. I had to experience it applied first. He was brilliant but also had a simple faith. He was quick to believe and quick to trust, even-tempered, compassionate. Not so with me. I so many times reacted then was sorry. Now that Bill is no longer here, I realize the balance. I made a choice to present Bill's manuscript to you as he wrote it and I did not change the voice to past tense. I did, however, insert a few comments to give you my perspective.

It is my prayer that by reading this book many will find the truest joy a human can know: living a life totally surrendered to almighty God.

Vonette Bright
Orlando, Florida

A NOTE FROM DR. BRIGHT

To many Western minds, the phrase "slaves of Jesus" is said to be a turn-off. The truth is, becoming slaves of Jesus is how we can "turn on" the power of God in our lives.

Of course, I certainly understand the need to record the strong biblical foundation for life with our Master, and I am delighted to share what this lifetime has taught me. I invite you to take a journey with me into the ultimate dimension of living—of being a royal slave of the King of kings!

Choice Point
Conduct yourself as if He were arriving at any moment.

1

THE ULTIMATE CHOICE

Choice Point
Love your Master first and above all other interests.

Their joy surprised me. The radiant countenances of more than 300 faces greeted me as I walked into a party at a luxurious "barn" on the ranch of a famous Hollywood movie star. The facility was attractive, and the *hors d'oeuvres* were sumptuous. The smiling faces struck me in a profound way, because I had never seen anything like them in the so-called Christian world of my upbringing. Of course, as a businessman, I had looked for joy in making money, and I had found a lot of people who seemed happy spending it; I also had found that all but a few had regrets about the price their families paid for their financial success.

Yet here were all these young Hollywood starlets and handsome actors and college students reveling in something unidentified, until I found that the common reason for them being there was that they knew Jesus Christ! I noted, "These people are having a blast!"

Soon, I, too, discovered the source of the joy that Christians can know: trusting in and obeying the Lord Jesus Christ. This is the secret to knowing the joy of God in our life. Jesus said that if we love Him, we will obey Him. He promised that if we obey Him, He will show Himself in full reality to us. "I have told you this so that you will be filled with my joy. Yes, your joy will overflow!" (John 15:11).

What powerful and marvelous promises! Obedience to God releases His blessings and joy, here and hereafter. "If you keep My commandments, you will abide in My love; just as I have kept My Father's commandments and abide in His love. These things I have spoken to you so that My joy may be in you, and that your joy may be made full" (John 15:10-11, *NASB*).

We sing the old hymn "Trust and obey, for there's no other way to be happy in Jesus, but to trust and obey." However, that obedience seems rare in the Western world of the twenty-first century. Humbling acts of service to others, as Jesus modeled when He washed the feet of His disciples, release joy in our hearts. Fellowships of caring Christians in community can be the most exciting places on earth. Instead, as veteran evangelist Sumner Wemp said recently, "Pride, arrogance, a haughty look, and the 'I have need of nothing' attitude are killing our churches."

A Thought from Vonette

I have often said that I believe Bill Bright lived as perfect a life as is possible for a person to live. He lived what he preached. He was not perfect, and I confess I reminded him of that from time to time. I have shared this statement more in recent years with our staff family. Now that Bill has left us, I want them to know the man he really was. It is not my desire to build up the person of Bill Bright, but as an example of the quality of life God offers and the possibilities of personal commitment.

What is so hard about obeying? Apparently, it is self-absorption. Western culture promotes self-sufficiency, self-reliance and self-pride. There is even a magazine in the U.S. entitled *Self.* An entire era has been named the "Me Generation" due to its selfishness. Greed and materialism romp through boardrooms, our government and, tragically, even some churches and ministries.

Selflessly obeying God is a liberating delight when we decide to see ourselves the way early followers of Jesus Christ saw themselves—*as His slaves!* The more we recognize that we can trust Him with everything, the more we obey, the more we love and the more joy we experience. Voluntary spiritual slavery thrives as "an important New Testament concept . . . in becoming slaves subject to the will of God, we become what God intended for us to be." This one idea captured us in 1951, when my beloved Vonette and I signed our contract with God. In it, we chose to place everything we were and all that we possessed under His ownership. We decided to recognize that we should live our lives as "slaves of Jesus."

We did it of our own free will, and it has been the most liberating and joyful decision we have ever made, apart from our salvation. This decision, far from being a life of rules and regulations and legalism, is based on how wonderfully trustworthy our Master is. He frees us to serve Him gladly in the joy and excitement of His resurrection. The idea of signing a contract to become slaves of Christ was not a concept we had heard from others; it was an experience of the heart based on our Lord's example in Philippians 2:7: "He made himself nothing; he took the humble position of a slave and appeared in human form."

For me, the contract came after more than two years of headlong zeal in following Jesus. After I had received the Lord, I became more and more busy for Him. I was running a successful business, going to seminary and was involved in nearly every aspect of the Hollywood Presbyterian Church, sometimes six and seven days a week. I was motivated by the love of Christ; but in all candor, joy in my spirit was not a constant experience. I would experience joy when someone prayed to receive Christ, when a task was done, when singing God's praises in the sanctuary or special gatherings and, of course, when our prayers were answered.

I had grown up in a ranching community where hard work was the mark of a person, where dawn to nightfall was the schedule. So, in Hollywood, along with some friends in the church, in sincere dedication of my life, I had worked hard to help compile a list of dos and don'ts of the Christian life. I soon discovered that I could not and did not perform them. With 20/20 hindsight, I can now say that I should have been praying, along with David, Lord, "restore to me again the joy of your salvation" (Ps. 51:12), rather than depending on my good, hard work.

I am saddened to say that I see these same kinds of legalistic rituals played out in far too many lives today. Striving to do things for God in the flesh is a trap. Formulas do not bring joy. Only the precious Holy Spirit can produce true joy. As long as our ideas, our dead works and our plans are driving us, we will know little joy.

But, dear friend, there is a fountain of joy to be released in our lives. It burst forth with Vonette and me as we decided to become slaves by choice of our magnificent Master, Savior and Friend, the Lord Jesus Christ.

A Thought from Vonette

It was a great privilege to share in this man's life. To watch him grow, face adversity and surrender his all. He inspired me in his commitment, and I felt safe in his leadership. I learned to trust his judgment—not blindly, I asked many questions and I often challenged him just to test his decisions and to be sure he had considered various points of view, and to be sure he had heard from God, not just his own wisdom. He was patient with me and brought me along. When I was sure of his stand, I could follow him enthusiastically.

The Voluntary Choice

Our son Zac, pastor of Divine Savior Presbyterian Church and leader in the Southern California C. S. Lewis Society, reminded me of how clearly American recording artist Bob Dylan described our choice in his album *Slow Train Coming*. Dylan wrote a song titled "Gotta Serve Somebody." He suggested, "Well, it may be the devil or it may be the Lord, but you're gonna have to serve somebody. . . . You may be a businessman or a high-degree thief. They may call you Doctor or they may call you Chief. . . . You may be rich or poor, you may be blind or lame, you may live in another country under another name. . . . But no matter what you say, you're gonna have to serve somebody, yes indeed, you're gonna have to serve somebody."[1]

Choosing to subordinate our will to that of others often makes our rebellious hearts cringe. We would rather, as Frank Sinatra sang, favor the pride of being able to say "I Did It My Way." Our egos may want the recognition given to Mother Teresa, the saint of Calcutta, but do we want to take orders to go into the streets with starving, diseased masses?

My saintly mother would frequently remind me, "You are no better or worse than anyone else." That stayed in my mind as a guidepost in social settings. I learned from my father that "your word is as good as your bond." This, too, became part of the governing ideas of my life. In like manner, I have thought of myself as "a slave of Jesus," and it has provided wonderful guidance.

Some have asked me to stop this "slave" self-description or deemphasize it, because of the heinous evil of human slavery. Of course, human slavery is morally wrong, ungodly, un-Christian and to be opposed at every opportunity. The two commitments (to Christ or to the practice of human slavery) cannot coexist in the same heart and mind and soul. When slave trader John Newton met Christ, not only did he stop trading in human lives, but he also began a life of preaching the truth of God's Word. This is why followers of Christ began and won the battle for the abolition of slavery in Western civilization. Fearless preachers of the gospel of Jesus Christ, like William Wilberforce, proclaimed the truth of the Bible, opposed slavery, and helped bring an end to this abominable practice (see Gal. 3:28; Eph. 2:14). That war is still being waged today in many developing countries (see appendix D).

Please remember that American slavery was *in*voluntary; it was forced upon dear people who in no way were given a *choice* to become slaves, and their masters were in no way anything like the blessed Master of our souls, our Lord Jesus Christ. By contrast, I have found *voluntary spiritual slavery* to the Lord Jesus to be *totally liberating*.

Others agree with me. Once, while in Rome, an outstanding national Christian leader had heard my description of deciding to be a slave of Jesus. He was traveling alone. The Holy Spirit seemed to impress him to make a formal decision. As he was walking near a place where there was a statue of Jesus, he experienced a divine compulsion to kneel in front of that statue, not because of its earthly value but because it drew his heart into focus on the Lord Jesus. Later, he told me: "I prayed, 'Lord, I want to be Your slave. Use me any way You wish. You are my God, my Savior, my Lord and now my Master.'" He said the decision lifted his life into a new dimension of joy and service.

Many believers are slaves of Jesus and do not know it. I have asked Christians, "Do you want your attitudes, actions and will to obey the Lord Jesus in all things?" Many are quick to say an emphatic yes. Then I ask, "Are you ready to love, trust and obey Him no matter what?" Again, they say yes. Now, that is the attitude and heart of a slave of Jesus! But when I ask, "Have you ever thought of yourself as a slave of Jesus?" the answer is usually, "I never thought of it that way."

A Litmus Test

Choosing to be a slave by choice has been a quick way for me to test my motives and my heart as to whether I am totally surrendered to God. We can check ourselves by simply asking the question: *Would a slave of Jesus think this way or act this way?* This question makes it easier to ignore countless temptations, because slaves of Jesus do not do that. By being occupied with the Master's words, we can dismiss thousands of selfish thoughts. By recognizing that we are the property of our Lord who lived so simply, we learn to live for Him, not live for acquiring things.

You can use joy as a test of your walk as a follower of Christ. Paul said three things would always remain: faith, hope and love (see 1 Cor. 13:13). We experience joy as we place our *faith* in the great God of creation and Calvary; He has everything under control, so we can relax and rejoice even while we work day and night for Him. We experience joy as we rest in the *hope* (the assurance and expectation) of His return. So we need no list, only the question: Am I ready for Him to come today? We experience joy as we let His *love* celebrate within us His finished work at the cross and His outworking of His will in our lives; so we rejoice in loving Him for all He has done and is doing.

The self-discipline that flows from being a slave of Jesus puts me where I belong—at the feet of the great Creator-God and Savior, Jesus Christ. He owns my life. He is responsible for all that happens to me. As I daily thank Him for His wonderful mastery, He reigns supreme and I am enriched by the glory of His presence, the grace of His provision, and the power of His love. There is no better way to live than by making the decision to be a slave of Jesus!

Controlled by the Spirit

In no way do I want to suggest that legalism in any form is a path to fruitful and spiritual living. In Zechariah 4:6, we are told, "It is not by force nor by strength, but by my Spirit, says the LORD Almighty." Part of the fruit of the Holy Spirit (see Gal. 5:22-23) is self-control. It is only through being filled, controlled and empowered by the Holy Spirit that we are able to experience the grace to operate as slaves of Jesus, to have our minds disciplined to love, trust and obey Him in all things and at all times.

A THOUGHT FROM VONETTE

The Christian lifestyle is not characterized by legalistic dos and don'ts; it is positive, attractive and joyful. Compare the experiences of the disciples with those of the Pharisees who tried to do God's will in their own strength and wisdom. The Pharisees always seemed to be waiting around, trying to catch someone breaking their religious laws. Jesus and the disciples always seemed to be touching people's hearts and lightening their burdens. There's no doubt about which group of people experienced the true adventure of servanthood.

To illustrate how to apply the "slave by choice" concept, consider the four keys to faith-filled living found in Romans 6. Thinking of myself as a slave of Jesus makes this process easier.

I know my position in Christ with all the duty and delight that brings. "Our old sinful selves were crucified with Christ so that sin might lose its power in our lives. We are no longer slaves to sin. For when we died with Christ we were set free from the power of sin" (Rom. 6:6-8). Now we can rejoice as we share His resurrection life in us (see v. 9).

I can move forward by faith in the fact that I am in Christ's royal household, with all the privileges that brings.

I give up my life to the wishes and requests of the Master.

I've made my choice. I do not think twice about obeying; it is the logical and natural thing to do, especially when the Master is the matchless and magnificent, loving Creator-God and Savior of our souls, the Lord Jesus Christ!

We Are All Slaves

Some may bristle at the word "slave" in any sense; but our Lord Jesus Christ used it as a word picture of spiritual behavior: "I tell you the truth, everyone who sins is a slave to sin" (John 8:34, *NIV*).

So the question of life is not *whether* we are slaves, but *whose* slaves are we? What has you enslaved? Perhaps you are a great money manager, but you are a control-slave: You will do anything to be in charge. Some are slaves to their cars, their houses and their gardens. Some are slaves to cocaine, marijuana or sex. Others are mastered by power or fame. Millions are slaves to debt, using their credit cards in impulse buying at the mall or on the Internet. Is your master Visa, or MasterCard? Throughout the earth, financial debt is the master of millions. Its tyranny controls lives.

Every generation has had those who spent beyond their means and found themselves enslaved, imprisoned and under the total domination of others because of debt. In the world in which our Lord Jesus grew and ministered, debt-slaves were everywhere. One scholar estimates that as many as 4 out of 10 residents of Rome, from AD 1 to AD 300, were slaves of one type or the other. Many of these were enslaved because they owed debts to their masters, and those masters kept them enslaved by charging high interest rates.

It was in that context that the apostle Paul lived and used the "slave" word picture to motivate believers to totally surrender their lives to Jesus.

The Slave Theme of the New Testament

The apostle Paul insisted he was a slave of Jesus: "I, Paul, am a devoted slave of Jesus Christ on assignment, authorized as an apostle to proclaim God's words and acts" (Rom. 1:1, *THE MESSAGE*). However, as the *Wycliffe Bible* commentators have noted, "The word for servant really means a slave. For Paul, this expression said that he belonged to Jesus Christ. He was Christ's property, and as such, he had a divinely appointed task to perform."

Paul was not alone in seeing himself this way. John the Baptist saw himself as *less* than a slave of Jesus: "I baptize with water those who turn from their sins and turn to God. But someone is coming soon who is far greater than I am—so much greater that I am not even worthy to be his slave. He will baptize you with the Holy Spirit and with fire" (Matt. 3:11).

James, Peter, Timothy, Epaphras and Jude specifically called themselves slaves (see Jas. 1:1; 2 Pet. 1:1; Col. 4:12; Jude 1:1), as did most early followers of our Lord. Paul wrote to the slave-rich city of Rome:

> And so, dear brothers and sisters, I plead with you to give your bodies to God. Let them be a living and holy sacrifice—the kind he will accept. When you think of what he has done for you, is this too much to ask? Don't copy the behavior and customs of this world, but let God transform you into a new person by changing the way you think. Then you will know what God wants you to do, and you will know how good and pleasing and perfect his will really is (Rom. 12:1-2).

Paul summarized his view of voluntary spiritual slavery:

> Don't you realize that whatever you choose to obey becomes your master? You can choose sin, which leads to death, or you can choose to obey God and receive his approval. Thank God! Once you were slaves of sin, but now you have obeyed with all your heart the new teaching

God has given you. Now you are free from sin, your old master, and you *have become slaves to your new master, righteousness* (Rom. 6:16-18, emphasis added).

A Living Illustration

"I speak this way," Paul said, "using the illustration of slaves and masters, because it is easy to understand. Before, you let yourselves be slaves of impurity and lawlessness. Now you must choose to be slaves of righteousness so that you will become holy. In those days, when you were slaves of sin, you weren't concerned with doing what was right. And what was the result? It was not good, since now you are ashamed of the things you used to do, things that end in eternal doom. But now you are free from the power of sin and have become *slaves of God*. Now you do those things that lead to holiness and result in eternal life. For the wages of sin is death, but the free gift of God is eternal life through Christ Jesus our Lord" (Rom. 6:19-23).

This one idea changed Paul's motives for living. He taught it: "If you were free when the Lord called you, you are now a slave of Christ" (1 Cor. 7: 22). He practiced it: "Do you think I speak this strongly in order to manipulate crowds? Or curry favor with God? Or get popular applause? If my goal was popularity, I wouldn't bother being Christ's slave" (Gal. 1:10, *THE MESSAGE*). He did so because he saw the example of Jesus as that of a sovereign king becoming a simple slave.

The Essence of the Word *Doulos*

Many modern translations have chosen to use the words "servant" or "bond-servant" instead of slave. Once, I was invited into a meeting where scholars were translating the New Testament for a new version of the Bible. They happened to be conferring that day about one word, *doulos,* the Greek word that occurs 141 times in the Bible. The primary debate was whether to translate the word "slave" or "bond-servant." I was asked my opinion, and I urged the translation to be "slave."

My main reason was the weakness of the church of our Lord Jesus in many places due to lack of complete surrender and ultimate commitment by His followers (see Eph. 2:10). In fact, once strong words such as "dedication" and "consecration," "conviction" and "commitment" seem to have withered into mere lip service in far too many places. In America, for example, it can be easier to join a church than to join a civic club. *Jesus made simple faith the basis for entry into His family, but He made revolutionary demands upon His followers* wrapped in a powerful challenge: "If you love me, obey my commandments" (John 14:15). He was the first to raise the issue of spiritual slavery (see John 8:34). And this is His command to all who will truly follow Him:

> Then he called his disciples and the crowds to come over and listen. "If any of you wants to be my follower," he told them, "you must put aside your selfish ambition, shoulder your cross, and follow me. If you try to keep your life for yourself, you will lose it. But if you give up your life for my sake and for the sake of the Good News, you will find true life. And how do you benefit if you gain the whole world but lose your own soul in the process? Is anything worth more than your soul? If a person is ashamed of me and my message in these adulterous and sinful days, I, the Son of Man, will be ashamed of that person when I return in the glory of my Father with the holy angels" (Mark 8:34-38).

The Greek language definitely permits, if not prefers, the translation as "slave." In the context of the culture of the Roman first century, slavery of all kinds was so common that the word was a very down-to-earth picture for communicating lifelong commitment. The word "servant" actually diminishes the portrait of a Christian commitment. In the first century, a true slave often became an accepted part of the owner's household. The term "bondservant" referred to those "slaves for a season" who could work off their bond or debt and resume living according to their own dictates, turning their backs to the master because of their works. I believe that picture does not adequately portray the pure grace by which we come to know the Lord Jesus as Savior (see Eph. 2:8-9), nor our response to His command to deny ourselves in full surrender to His Lordship of our lives.

The Bible definition of *doulos,* according to *Strong's Greek Lexical Parser,* is as follows:

> (1) a slave, bondman, man of servile condition; (1a) a slave; (1b) metaphor for one who gives himself up to another's will whose service is used by Christ in extending and advancing His cause among men; (1c) devoted to another to the disregard of one's own interests.[2]

In the earliest manuscripts of the New Testament, *doulos* is used not only to denote slaves of human masters, but also to describe *kings and prophets* as slaves of the Lord. So, we can surmise that Paul's description of himself as a slave of Christ was intended to have two meanings: (1) He signals his understanding of the servant nature of following Jesus; (2) he also cites "the special privilege of belonging to Jesus," as would one of the imperial slaves in the courts of Roman leaders.

In addition, Paul speaks of himself as the slave of his converts (see 2 Cor. 4:5) and of those to whom he preached the gospel (see 1 Cor. 9:19). This was a matter of both heart and mind to him; he wanted to serve others because of the love he had experienced from Christ. But he did not choose to allow others to be his *master.* He declared that he was bound to only one Master, our Lord Jesus Christ, and he served others only as a result of his allegiance to Jesus (see 2 Cor. 4:5).

The Result of Voluntary Slavery

Voluntary slavery to Jesus produces immense satisfaction. It leads to our choosing to rest in the position of being under godly authority in all areas of our lives: husband and wife mutually surrendered to God; family submitted to the leadership of pastor and church; and citizens obeying godly laws.

This idea of *voluntary* total surrender and self-denial is what our Lord Jesus asks of those who follow Him. It is enlistment to obey the Master in what appears to the world to be extreme service. The profound difference, of course, is that we are surrendering control to Jesus Christ, who is our great Creator-God and Savior who calls us to love Him and to love others as ourselves.

Choosing to think of myself as a slave of Jesus has changed my life. My prayer is that you will consider making the same decision. If you do, based on the promises of God, I believe you will experience the same liberation and joy I have known and still experience to this very day.

Since our decision, Vonette and I have spoken both privately and publicly of what it is like to be a "slave by choice." The Bible says, "As he thinks within himself, so is he" (Prov. 23:7, *NASB*). In like manner, as I have thought of myself as "a slave of Jesus," I have been freed from all other forces or persons who would seek to possess and control me.

Admittedly, our decision to recognize Jesus as Master of all did not come in a flash. It was after I had enjoyed worldly interests and business success as a non-believing materialist. I had my share of conflicts and controversy. Later, I became a Christian and had become religious, going to church virtually every time the doors were open. But it was not until I became completely enthralled by the captivating love of God for me that I came to the end of myself and realized there was only one way to be free: enslavement to the most liberating Person in history!

As a businessman, I decided it was time to sell everything to the Lord Jesus, as they say, "lock, stock and barrel!" We, in effect, turned over the title deed of our lives. Vonette and I even chose the use of a written contract as a way of concretely stating our hearts' desire to allow Jesus to be Owner of All. In my heart, I was thinking, *Lord, You are the Master of my life; all I own or ever hope to own is Yours; all I am or ever hope to be is Yours; You bought me, I am Your slave. I trust You to take care of me, because I know, now, how much You love me.*

Signed Contracts with the Master

Vonette and I each literally signed the contract with our Lord to be His slaves. We specified that we understood that He owned us and all we had. We surrendered our lives to His decision and control. I know now, with the benefit of hindsight, that this decision was merely a way for me to recognize the joy of what theologians call "spiritual slavery." It is the beginning of the outworking of the joy of our salvation (see Phil. 2:12). I journeyed from being the master of my own fate to realizing the enormity of God's love and incredible plan for my life and wanting to serve Him completely and forever. I wanted to be a slave to such a wonderful Master!

Approximately 24 hours later, I received an overwhelming awareness of how God might use me to help fulfill the Great Commission in my lifetime. This vision quickly led Vonette and me to found Campus Crusade for Christ. Let me offer a word of caution. God did not say, "Let's make a deal: Become a slave and I'll give you a worldwide ministry." What my spirit felt was more like this:

> Master, You love me so much; You are so powerful and wonderful. I want to serve only You all the days of my life. Your word is my command. I surrender everything to Your ownership and direction. I choose to be Your slave; do with me as You will and I will praise You all the days of my life. I decided to be bound to Him forever, with no way of getting out of that decision, unless I wanted to break my word; and I did not intend to do that . . . ever. I am convinced, "No contract, no vision."

Quietly but resolutely seeing myself as a slave of Jesus has produced more *freedom, faith* and *fruit* than I could ever have imagined. The concept of being a slave of Jesus came to me from the experience of Jesus (see Phil. 2:7) and the writings of the apostle Paul (see Rom. 1:1).

"In becoming slaves, subject to the will of God, we become what God intended us to be," says Dr. Lawrence O. Richards, scholar and former professor at Wheaton College. "The believer finds freedom, not in recovering an independent will, but in submitting his will freely and joyfully to God. . . . Jesus has paid the purchase price and freed us from the deadly power of sin. He has taken us into His household, and now we find our destiny by accepting His lordship."[3]

That is why Paul used the "slave" word picture to motivate believers to totally surrender their lives to Jesus. His listeners and readers could readily identify debt with slavery. When they also understood his message of the liberating love of Jesus, their hearts captured the point: Being enslaved to money does not pay off in time or eternity, but being a slave of Jesus does!

In the U.S. today, the WWJD phenomenon conveys well what it means to be a slave of Jesus. Asking What Would Jesus Do? has become a popular way for Christians to identify with their Master. They wear bracelets, engrave wallets, sport license plates, and use other ways to send the message that they will be guided by following the example of the Lord Jesus and pausing to think of His commands and promises. If only we all would sincerely seek this kind of obedience, the resulting joy would set off a powerful spiritual revolution!

Steve Douglass, the president of Campus Crusade for Christ International, whose love for our Lord and leadership in the global Body of Christ has blessed me so much, once asked me a question in a radio interview. "We all die sometime," he said. "When that happens to you, how would you hope that you'd be remembered?"

I replied, "As a slave of Jesus." There's no higher privilege—to be crucified with Christ, to be raised with Him, to be seated with Him in the heavenlies. I wanted, originally, to have an unmarked grave, but Vonette didn't think that was a good idea. So, we decided that we would have a tombstone on which would be written our names, "Slaves of Jesus, A life lived well/ William R. Bright/ October 19, 1921–July 19, 2003/A Slave of Jesus by Choice," with references to the fact of Philippians 2:7 (the Lord Jesus was a slave); Romans 1:1 (Paul was a slave); Peter was a slave; and so on, and challenge everyone who visits the cemetery to become "slaves of Jesus."

The Ultimate Choice

Becoming a "slave by choice" for Jesus means committing one's self to serving Him completely. In the following sections, first discover what God's Word says about being a slave to Jesus (His choice), and then make the choices to experience the joy of serving Jesus (my choice). Read each verse and carefully answer the questions.

His Choice

What is the relationship between obedience and joy (see John 15:10-11)?

_____

_____

_____

_____

What was Jesus' relationship to others when He came to earth (see Phil. 2:5-8)?

_____

_____

_____

_____

What type of slavery should we avoid at all costs (see John 8:34)?

_____

_____

_____

_____

What common words do these passages use to describe these believers: James, Peter, Epaphras and Jude (see Jas. 1:1; 2 Pet. 1:1; Col. 4:12; Jude 1:1)?

_____

_____

_____

_____

My Choice

Proverbs 23:7 says about a person, "As he thinks within himself, so is he" (*NASB*). Prayerfully consider your thought life and priorities. What attitudes or habits tend to control your life? List at least three.

_____

_____

_____

_____

_____

Thinking about each of the items you wrote for the previous question, apply the Spiritual Litmus Test to each: "Would a slave of Jesus think or act this way?" Write a note next to each, describing how it measures up to being a slave of Jesus.

_____

_____

_____

_____

_____

If you have never considered yourself a slave of choice for Jesus before now, and you desire to deny yourself and follow Him completely, use the prayer of commitment in the chapter to tell Him.

Notes

1. Bob Dylan. *Slow Train Coming*, "You Gotta Serve Somebody." Copyright © 1979 Special Rider Music. All rights reserved. International copyright secured. Reprinted by permission.
2. *Strong's Greek Lexical Parser*, Greek #1401, s.v. "*doulous*."
3. Lawrence O. Richards, *New International Encyclopedia of Bible Words* (Grand Rapids, MI: Zondervan, 1991), p. 123.

I AM NOT MY OWN

Choice Point

Major in His meekness.

If you were a slave in the time of the early Christian Church, and many were, it might be said of you and your fellow slaves: "They have an attitude!" In a word, slaves were known for their *obedience.* Slaves obeyed, period. No hesitation, speeches or protests. Simply obedience.

Here are some of the characteristics of a slave in the Roman era:

- The slave was bound to the master in cords so strong that only death could break them.
- The slave served the master to the utter "disregard for his own interests."
- The slave's own will was engulfed in the will of the master.[1]

This image was impressively clear to the Roman world, which included many "royal slaves" whose masters were high officials. As a result, those slaves themselves enjoyed special privileges. Readers of the apostle Paul's letter to the Romans fully understood his message. In the culture of Rome, becoming a slave by choice of the Lord Jesus Christ was deciding to *be somebody*!

After all, it was the Lord Jesus who became history's first slave by choice. As a member of the Royal Household of Eternity, our Lord chose to come to earth disguised as a slave, obedient even when it tore at His very being (see Phil. 2:5,7). Jesus was in no way obligated to undertake such a mission. He realized fully what His choice meant: "Father, if you are willing, please take this cup of suffering away from me. Yet I want your will, not mine" (Luke 22:42). Even death would not keep Him from obeying His Father.

I also marvel at the obedience of Mary, the mother of Jesus, who submitted her will to be a slave (Greek *doule*) of the God who chose her. She said, "Behold, the bondslave of the Lord; may it be done to me according to your word" (Luke 1:38, *NASB*). In Luke 1:46-56, we see in her exemplary prayer (1) the heart attitude of a slave, (2) the slave's need of a Savior from sin's bondage, and (3) the blessing that comes from faithful obedience. She became an outstanding portrait of the virtues of being a slave by choice. As a result, in fact, she is called "blessed" by all generations.

We are missing out on some of the joy of the abundant life when we fail to celebrate and emulate the heart of Mary. She was obedient to God when she did not understand all that would happen to her. Of course, we know that "there is only one God and one Mediator who can reconcile God and humanity—the man Christ Jesus" (1 Tim. 2:5). But her prayer contains part of what ought to be in the heart of every follower of Christ: adoring our God, expecting Him to keep His promises, obeying His commands, resting in her position as a slave of God.

Salvation and Sanctification

I can relate to Paul's decision, and I seek to follow his example. His choice is one we all can make. He was heading one way—toward the praise and acceptance of others for the works that he thought would put him in good standing with God. He had all the credentials this world can offer. Then he met Jesus, and he was never the same. He gave up everything to be a slave of the most amazing Master of the universe. Few have summed up Paul's decision to be a slave by choice better than Greek-word scholar Kenneth Wuest:

> Paul was born a slave of sin at his physical birth, and a
> bondslave of his Lord's through regeneration (his spiri-
> tual rebirth). The cords that bound him to his old mas-

ter, Satan, were rent asunder (torn apart) in his identifi-
cation with Christ in the latter's death. The cords that
bind him to his new Master will never be broken since
the new Master will never die again, and is Paul's new
life. Paul's will, at one time swallowed up in the will of
Satan, now is swallowed up in the sweet will of God. The
reader will observe how wonderfully God has watched
over the development of the Greek language so that at
the time it was needed as the medium through which He
would give His New Testament to the human race, its
words were fit receptacles and efficient instruments for
the conveyance of His message to man. . . . *The apostle is
proud of the fact that he is a slave belonging to his Lord.* There
were certain individuals in the Roman Empire desig-
nated "Slaves of the Emperor." This was a position of
honor. One finds a reflection of this in Paul's act of des-
ignating himself as a slave of the King of kings. He puts
this ahead of his apostleship.[2]

This idea of voluntary total commitment is what our Lord Jesus asks of those who follow Him—not for a tour of duty but for
all of earth and eternity. It is enlistment to obey the Master in
what appears to the world to be extreme service. The profound
difference, of course, is that we are surrendering control not to a
government but to Jesus Christ, who is our great Creator-God
and Savior who calls us to love Him with all of our heart, soul,
mind and strength and others as ourselves (see Mark 12:29-31).

Identifying myself as a slave of Jesus has changed my life.
My prayer is that you will consider making the same decision, if
you have not already done so. If you do, based on the promises
of God, I am confident that you will experience the same liberation I have known and still experience to this very day.

In the next four chapters, we will see some of the characteristics of slaves of Jesus—as they relate to God, to a slave's inner self,
to others and to life in general. They include insights that help
guide a follower of Christ in decision-making. These have become

part of my ongoing thinking, and as a result they are some of the governing ideas of my life. As we shall see, believers think differently as they meditate on what it means to be a slave of Jesus.

I Am Not My Own

His Choice

What does it cost to be a slave of Jesus? Read each passage and describe the commitment and what it cost that person to be a slave for God.

Jesus

The commitment: Luke 22:39-46

_____

_____

_____

_____

The cost: John 19:16-18

_____

_____

_____

Mary

The commitment: Luke 1:38,46-49

_____

_____

_____

_____

The cost: John 19:25-27

_____

_____

_____

_____

Paul
The commitment: Romans 1:1

_____

_____

_____

_____

The cost: 2 Corinthians 12:8-9

_____

_____

_____

_____

My Choice

With the type of commitment seen in the lives of Mary and Paul,
you may wonder, _How can being a slave for Jesus bring joy?_ Read each
set of verses. After each passage, explain (1) the type of joy the
verse(s) mention and (2) what each means to you.

Romans 7:14-20

_____

_____

_____

_____

Nehemiah 8:10

_____

_____

_____

_____

Psalm 16:11

_____

_____

_____

_____

Romans 15:13

_____

_____

_____

_____

Galatians 5:22

_____

_____

_____

_____

1 Thessalonians 2:19-20

_____

_____

_____

_____

James 1:2-4

_____

_____

_____

_____

Notes

1. W. E. Vine, Merrill F. Unger, William White, Jr., *Vine's Complete Expository Dictionary of Old and New Testament Words* (Nashville: TN: Thomas Nelson, 1996).
2. Kenneth Wuest, *Wuest's Word Studies from the Greek New Testament* (Grand Rapids, MI: Wm. B. Eerdmans Publishing Co., 1975), Romans, emphasis added.

3

KNOWING GOD PERSONALLY

Choice Point
Guard against compromise.

"Dr. Bright, do you realize how many times you refer to yourself as a 'slave of Jesus,' especially when you are explaining a personal decision?"

The question caught me off guard. Certainly, when Vonette and I decided to sign contracts to be slaves of the Lord Jesus, it became a recurring reference point for us. And, through the years, as we share our testimonies, we often do observe that "slaves of Jesus" behave in a radically different way than the world commonly does. So I began to give thought to writing this book. How do slaves of Jesus think? What are their attributes? What characterizes their behavior—toward God, toward themselves, toward others, toward life?

Venture with me into some of the excitement and joy of choosing to become a slave of Jesus. Perhaps these insights will help you decide to adopt the same mindset that has guided Vonette and me during the past five decades. These truths can help guide your decision-making as you, too, seek to live a life of total surrender to our Lord.

I was an agnostic until I was confronted by the claims of Jesus of Nazareth, the Messiah. Jesus spoke and lived as no other in history. Uniquely, He claimed to have lived in eternity past before coming to earth. Jesus said, "The truth is, I existed before Abraham was even born" (John 8:58). He alone claimed to be God in the flesh: "The Father and I are one" (John 10:30). No sane person has ever even claimed that he did only what God the Father told him. No other person predicted his own death, burial and resurrection as atonement for the sins of all mankind. Only Jesus left His tomb empty in Jerusalem to appear to hundreds alive again, and then ascended to the throne of God, promising to return. Only Jesus claims to be the pathway to heaven: "I am the way, the truth, and the life; no one can come to the Father except through me" (John 14:6).

Slaves of Jesus serve an incomparable, peerless Master.

> *"For I, the Son of Man, am master. . . . There is only one master, the Messiah. . . . Who do you say I am?" (Matt. 12:8; 23:10; 16:15).*

How would you answer the question Jesus asked?

This presents us with what has been called "the great trilemma": Jesus is either Lord (who He claimed to be as God in the flesh), or He is the greatest liar and impostor of all time, or He is a lunatic whose mind left Him long ago and far away! The intellectual problem He poses stems from the fact that Jesus did not *live* as if He were a fraud or mentally ill. To the contrary, everything He did while on earth attested that His claims to be God were true. He was tested as all humans, but never sinned. He forgave people their sins on His own authority. He healed the sick. He spoke as no other but said His words came "from the Father." He loved all of us so much that He sacrificed His life on a cruel Roman cross and rose from the grave that we might enjoy abundant life with Him forever.

This love and brilliance of the Savior captured me. Other masters demand personal sacrifice, but only Jesus *voluntarily sacrificed* for each of us. So I voluntarily chose to be yoked to Him, because He alone is worthy of my life's service. That choice does not make life easy. However, the troubles are nothing compared to the glory of knowing our Lord Jesus as Master of all we have and are. I was challenged to ask Him, as did the apostle Paul: "Lord, what would You have me to do?" That began the journey. Each day is another opportunity to ask the same question and obey the Master's reply.

Slaves of Jesus know God personally! We enjoy a daily walk with the greatest Person of all time and eternity. We hear, read, study, meditate and memorize His words so that we are fortified against frightening threats. We know that we are led by the greatest Leader in history, who has the tender patience of a shepherd with His sheep. We are cared for by the Creator who flung 100 billion galaxies into space. He has promised us heaven as our eternal home and has given us the Holy Spirit as our constant Companion to guide us through any and all circumstances of life. As we train our minds to think on Jesus, we have a steady heart full of praise and love for the greatest Master of eternity. He alone is worthy of our total surrender—of all that we are, all that we possess and all that we can ever hope to be. There is no one like Him in time and eternity!

Our Master's uniqueness makes Him alone worthy of our total surrender, service and praise.

A slave of Christ always looks forward, not yearning for the past.

If you love me, you will keep my commandments. . . . No one can serve two masters. For you will hate one and love the other, or be devoted to one and despise the other (John 16:15; Luke 16:13).

How many masters do I serve in my world?

The price of loving the Lord includes despising the values of the world system, our own selfish desires and the enemy of our souls, the evil one.

Stop loving this evil world and all that it offers you, for when you love the world, you show that you do not have the love of the Father in you. For the world offers only the lust for physical pleasure, the lust for everything we see, and pride in our possessions. These are not from the Father. They are from this evil world. And this world is fading away, along with everything it craves. But if you do the will of God, you will live forever (1 John 2:15-17).

Slaves of Jesus keep their hearts in love with God, and they detest sin. Each day, there is spirit, life and logic in obeying God's plans for our lives. We do not have to get deeply involved in a struggle to "figure some way out of this" or to strive for "special power to obey." Our Master is with us, right beside us; knowing this makes life's paths very clear: His way, our own way or someone else's way. Among those choices, only the way provided by Jesus the Master makes sense. He is the only Person I know who is worthy of my total allegiance and loyalty in all things, at all times.

Our Master will not share His slaves' loyalty with anyone else.

> *Your attitude should be the same that Christ Jesus had. Though he was God, he did not demand and cling to his rights as God. He made himself nothing; he took the humble position of a slave and appeared in human form (Phil. 2:5-7).*

Is there anyone or anything that I love more than I love Jesus?

He has earned our loyalty and complete devotion by His love and death on the cross. We dare not choose anything that would grieve His heart.

Have you ever made a serious effort to measure what Jesus gave up for you and for me? He had it all—authority, prominence, power, worship, riches and peace. He came from such heights and descended to such depths. If an eagle became a worm, we would be astonished. Yet infinitely greater, the King of all Creation became one of His creatures. Then He actually died for you and me, paying with His own human body and blood a ransom for our souls. This is astounding condescension—the best for the least, the King as slave and sacrifice!

The apostle Peter said that Jesus is our "example that we should follow in His steps." If we think as He demonstrated, we will barely think of ourselves at all. Our daily attitude will be one of obeying God's will for our lives, of giving ourselves in service to others, of sharing the love of Jesus with anyone we can . . . and not expect any special recognition on earth. We will not show off our power, wealth or authority; we will simply serve and tell everyone who will listen about Him.

Our Master set the example of sacrificial love for the world.

> *As slaves of Christ, do the will of God with all your heart . . . Come to me, all of you who are weary and carry heavy burdens, and I will give you rest. Take my yoke upon you. Let me teach you, because I am humble and gentle, and you will find rest for your souls. For my yoke fits perfectly, and the burden I give you is light (Eph. 6:6; Matt. 11:28-30).*

How much of what I do is sacrificing for others?

Slaves of Jesus have an attitude toward God that brings joy as we follow the ways of the Master. This attitude of humility keeps us out of prideful conflicts. This mindset keeps us serving those

He died for, regardless of the circumstances. We have no time for being judgmental or jealous; we are too busy obeying the Great Lover of our soul! This gives us a head start in devoting ourselves and our praise to the Lord and Master of all, today and tomorrow—ahead of everyone who one day will bow the knee before Him as the Ultimate Master of the universe. For me, having this mindset means greeting each morning with a prayer such as this: "Dear Savior, today walk around in my body, think with my mind, speak with my lips, touch with my hands and help me seek and save 'the lost.'" Encountering each day's activities this way, by faith, becomes an exciting adventure to see what God wants to do in and through us.

"How do you do it?" I am often asked. My answer often is: "Just give the load to the Lord Jesus, obey His commands, trust His promises and relax . . . while going 90 miles an hour!" I do not mean it as a joke; there really is a balance available to the slave of Jesus; we can serve with a glad heart and well-worn shoes! Showing up for work is my job. Accepting the assignment the Master gives me is my duty. But if my load is unreasonable and I cannot bear it with a joyful heart, it did not come from the Master! That is the moment to ask: (1) Have I taken the burden upon myself? (2) Did I let someone else place it upon me? (3) Am I struggling to perform the task in my own strength rather than relying on the Holy Spirit? Slaves focus only on the Master's assignments.

For example, I shall never forget the freedom I felt when I discovered that successful witnessing is simply taking the initiative to share the Person and claims of Christ, in the power of the Holy Spirit, and leaving the results to God. It revolutionized my life. All I had to do was obey the Master. I did not even have to create the message; I merely had to report what the Master has already said about Himself! If people were wise enough to accept His message, I was joyful for their obedience to His call. But if they did not respond, I was still joyful because I had obeyed by faith and trusted the Master to handle the results. I felt no rejection. I felt some sadness that they did not join me in wanting a personal relationship with our loving Lord and Savior at that time. But the freedom from any guilt in my own life remained! I was still saved by grace, not by works, and I was being obedient to my Master (see Eph. 2:8-10)!

Slaves of Jesus know the difference between pressure and stress. As we go, we cast all our cares on the Lord (see 1 Pet. 5:7). We know joy in service. As a result, we experience a radiant countenance and appealing witness. For some, life may be a funereal death-march; but for slaves of Jesus it is a joyous dance in the footsteps of the Master.

Our Master expects only what He enables us to do.

Humans can reproduce only human life, but the Holy Spirit gives new life from heaven (John 3:6).

Am I serving in the strength of the flesh or of the Spirit?

Focused Faithfulness

"Now after a long time the master of those slaves came and settled accounts with them" (Matt. 25:19, *NASB*). I do not want to be out of fellowship with our dear Lord even for one minute! Sin recognized must become sin confessed from the heart. Living this way liberates the mind, soul and spirit to be the authentic, creative people He made us to be.

Most of my early years I traveled so much that it became critical that much of my time at home needed to be spent serving my own family faithfully. Vonette and the boys would have serious to-do lists for me upon my return. I can remember Vonette going out one day and assigning me something to finish before her return. I do not remember exactly the task. What I recall is this: When she returned, I had NOT done it! That was a feeling I sought to avoid forevermore! I was without excuse; I had become distracted by other jobs and telephone calls.

The Lord Jesus looks for focused faithfulness on the job, working HIS priorities. He is returning at any time, and when He does, I need to be at my post, serving as He assigned me. He promises promotions for this kind of service, but they do not motivate me; His love does.

Slaves of Jesus have new authority and new responsibility as we love, trust and obey the Master's commands. A day of reckoning lies ahead when He will examine our stewardship. The more we settle here on earth, the less we will face on that day of reckoning. "His master said to him, 'Well done, good and faithful slave, you were faithful with a few things, I will put you in charge of many things, enter into the joy of your master'" (Matt. 25:23, *NASB*).

Our Master rejoices over a focused, faithful slave.

> *But if that slave says in his heart, "My master will be a long time in coming," and begins to beat the slaves, both men and women, and to eat and drink and get drunk; the master of that slave will come on a day when he does not expect him and at an hour he does not know, and will cut him in pieces, and assign him a place with the unbelievers. And that slave who knew his master's will and did not get ready or act in accord with his will, will receive many lashes (Luke 12:45-48, NASB).*

Whose agenda controls my day?

I must live moment by moment in the delight of this good news: He is coming! Slipping into "neutral" while on the drive of my life will make me late and absent. Until our Master returns, I must give Him my *best*, and not merely do enough to get by. The Lord Jesus has let His will be known, and if we fail to do it, there will be consequences (see Heb. 12:4-6). Staying aware of His return alters our behavior. We live and work so that we will not be embarrassed at the moment of His return.

Slaves of Jesus live responsibly. Rather than leaning back and settling for the second-class and second-rate, they stay on their toes, aiming for excellence. His imminent return gives even further motivation to stay focused on the mission and purpose of our lives. Whether our lives seem menial or majestic to others makes no difference; we live in light of the examining eye of the King of kings.

Our Master has given His slaves their marching orders until He returns.

> *Then the officer said, "Lord, I am not worthy to have you come into my home. Just say the word from where you are, and my servant will be healed! I know, because I am under the authority of my superior officers and I have authority over my soldiers. I only need to say, 'Go,' and they go, or 'Come,' and they come. And if I say to my slaves, 'Do this or that,' they do it." When Jesus heard this, he was amazed. Turning to the crowd, he said, "I tell you the truth, I haven't seen faith like this in all the land of Israel!" (Matt. 8:8-10).*

If Jesus returned today, would I hear Him say, "Well done, good and faithful slave"?

Whose word do we take as the controlling authority in our lives? And how long do we wait before we act on that word? Wasted time can be a sign of misplaced faith. The anxious worry "What if?" and spend hours in the paralysis of analysis. By choice and by faith,

I can simply obey what I already know to be the commands and will of my Master: Love God, love one another. . . . Love your enemies. . . . Do good to all, especially the household of faith. "I have been given complete authority in heaven and on earth. Therefore, go and make disciples of all the nations, baptizing them in the name of the Father and the Son and the Holy Spirit. Teach these new disciples to obey all the commands I have given you. And be sure of this: I am with you always, even to the end of the age" (Matt. 28:18-20).

Those are tall orders, and they are always in force! Don't fret, worry or wring your hands. Instead, obey whatever He has commanded! Military commanders know that success in war is not only gauged by how much armed force they may possess, but also by how much power they can deliver in a timely way to each battle! Within hours after receiving God's vision for Vonette and me, I felt compelled to drop my seminary labors immediately and begin the ministry of Campus Crusade for Christ, even though I had five years of study invested. The Master had spoken, and my duty was to submit to His authority and go!

Our Master expects His slaves to respond promptly to Him.

When you obey me, you remain in my love, just as I obey my Father and remain in his love (John 15:10-11).

If delayed obedience constitutes disobedience, how obedient to God am I?

Slaves of Jesus know the satisfaction of promptly obeying the authority of His Word in directing their lives. We know the joy of time well spent! We have clear priorities. We have an assurance that His will is being done to the extent we know and understand.

Our job is to obey what we know the Master wants done now, and we can trust Him for all other matters to be handled in His time. Even more, we know the Lord delights in our acting in faith at the very mention of His command!

Through the years, in all matters of obedience, I have learned that it can be dangerous to seek to obey in our own strength. I have sought to live according to Philippians 2:13: "It is God who is at work in you, both to will and to work for His good pleasure" (*NASB*). Whatever He leads me to do, He will enable me to do! With the hymn writer, we can declare: "Christ the Royal Master leads against the foe; forward into battle, see His banner go!"[1] All praise be to our matchless Supreme Commander of the Universe!

Knowing God Personally

His Choice

Our attitudes usually come from the way we reason and feel about life. From the following verses, find the reasons why we serve Jesus with all of our heart.

Matthew 23:10—This verse gives the foundation for our relationship with Jesus. What is it?

_____

_____

_____

_____

_____

_____

John 8:58—What is one of the reasons we serve Jesus?

_____

_____

_____

_____

_____

_____

John 14:6—What is another reason we serve Jesus?

_____
_____
_____
_____
_____
_____

John 15:5—What is a third reason we serve Jesus?

_____
_____
_____
_____
_____

My Choice

Because of who our Master is, we will serve Him in any way possible. After reading the following verses and prayerfully considering the attitude each presents, write down one way you can apply this attitude to your daily life.

John 16:27—Love the Master most of all.

_____
_____
_____
_____
_____

Philippians 2:5-7—Adopt a selfless mindset.

_____
_____
_____
_____
_____

Matthew 11:28-30—Learn from Jesus.

_____
_____
_____
_____

Matthew 25:23—Obey faithfully to please Jesus.

_____
_____
_____
_____

Matthew 25:1-13—Anxiously look for His return to earth.

_____
_____
_____
_____

Matthew 8:8-10—Respond promptly.

_____
_____
_____
_____

Note
1, "Onward Christian Soldiers," Sabine Baring-Gould (1834–1924).

4

TRUE HUMILITY

Choice Point
*Gain favor as you do what you can under the
direction of your Master.*

The famous cartoon character *Pogo* once said, "We have met the
enemy, and he is us!" The wonderful and horrible capacities
that reside within the human heart still boggle my mind. The
Lord Jesus said, "For from within, out of a person's heart, come
evil thoughts, sexual immorality, theft, murder, adultery, greed,
wickedness, deceit, eagerness for lustful pleasure, envy, slander,
pride, and foolishness" (Mark 7:21-22).

To be a disciple of our Lord Jesus, we must heed His strong
word: "If any of you wants to be my follower, you must *put aside
your selfish ambition*, shoulder your cross, and follow me" (Matt.
16:24, emphasis added).

God does not want to destroy our personality and individ-
uality. But He wants us to surrender our will to Him. John the
Baptist understood the issue when he said, "He [Jesus] must become greater and greater, and I must become less and less"
(John 3:30).

The apostle Paul explains the matter with a paradox: "I myself no longer live, but Christ lives in me. So I live my life in this
earthly body by trusting in the Son of God, who loved me and
gave himself for me" (Gal. 2:20).

Christians practice self-examination to double-check for
possibly selfish motives. This is personal business. It is so

important that it even can affect our health. Paul admonished the Corinthian Christians that many of them were sick and near death because they had not assessed the sin in their lives and were subject to the judgment of God (see 1 Cor. 11:27-32). This inward analysis was one of the reasons given for our taking part in the Lord's Supper remembrance of what Christ has done for us, and to remember the things He has told us to do.

Our Master expects His slaves to respond promptly to Him.

> *No one can serve two masters. For you will hate one and love the other, or be devoted to one and despise the other. You cannot serve both God and money. . . . A double-minded man [is] unstable in all his ways. . . . For the love of money is at the root of all kinds of evil (Luke 16:13; Jas. 1:8, NASB; 1 Tim. 6:10).*

If delayed obedience is disobedience, how obedient to God am I?

I was a complete materialist. You name it, I wanted it. The best cars, houses, land, clothes and meals were my everyday goals. I even promised Vonette, when I proposed to her, that she would live like a queen in prestigious Bel Air, California. I said we would travel often around the world. But as I grew in my faith in Christ, I realized that our Lord does not want material gain to be the focus of our lives. He wants to protect us from our tendency to serve wealth and to suffer the pangs it can bring. So Vonette and I chose Him over wealth as the driving force in our lives. We decided to believe His promise that all our basic needs will be supplied if we "seek first the kingdom of God and His righteousness" (Matt. 6:33, *ESV*).

A Thought from Vonette

Just to give you a glimpse of the practical side of our chosen lifestyle, I want to tell you how wonderfully God provided for my domestic needs. It seemed that daily we had people in our home to minister to and, frequently, groups of people staying with us. One particular weekend, we had three couples staying with us. Earlier I had been given a well-used six-burner hotel stove. I thought that large stove was wonderful, but my joy began to fade as one by one the burners stopped working while I was preparing a meal for our guests. I announced to our guests that dinner would be a bit later than planned since I was cooking with one burner.

Soon after that weekend, I received a call from the treasurer of Campus Crusade who instructed me to purchase a new stove and portable dishwasher. Someone's generosity had met my need.

You may wonder why I would tell you this example. I would like you to consider the responsiveness of the person who met my need as an act of obedience to what God prompted that person to do.

Jesus said, "Don't store up treasures here on earth, where they can be eaten by moths and get rusty, and where thieves break in and steal. Store your treasures in heaven, where they will never become moth eaten or rusty and where they will be safe from thieves" (Matt. 6:19-20).

Soon, the things of this world began to fade from the focus of our hearts. For example, we found ourselves saying no, even to a gracious offer from an automobile dealer friend to let us drive a brand-new, expensive "loaner." We had dependable transportation and that was all we really needed. As we made these decisions, God did not respond to our choices with a devious "Gotcha! Now, you'll live in slums forever." To the contrary, He has blessed us with all that we need and more.

As slaves of Jesus, we make serving Christ our priority and let the Holy Spirit guide us. We experience many immediate benefits of forsaking materialism. Here are a few: We avoid the frustrations that come from living life with loyalties divided between money or the Master. That issue is settled! This helps steer us past financial conflicts of interest because the Master owns everything! We have stability of purpose because our motives are not drawn away from the mission of our lives. We serve with a single, pure motive—to love and follow Jesus. We have obvious directions and commands from the Master in His Word. All this puts greed in its place, far outside the control room of our lives. Money is not a throne to be worshiped; it is merely a tool to use in our little vineyard of His kingdom.

Our Master expects us to use all our resources for His glory.

> *You call me Teacher and Lord, and you say well, for I am. If I then, your Lord and Teacher, have washed your feet, you also ought to wash one another's feet. For I have given you an example, that you should do as I have done to you. Most assuredly, I say to you, a servant is not greater than his master; nor is he who sent greater than he that sent him. . . . If you understand what I'm telling you, act like it—and live a blessed life (John 13:13-16, NKJV; John 13:17, THE MESSAGE).*

Am I letting the Lord use my God-given assets for His kingdom?

Humility is an unusual quality. When you think you have it, you probably do not! It comes as much by dedicated perspiration as by inspiration—mainly from following the Master's example in dealing with people. He came from such heights and bent so low, a King born in a stable, the Royal Master washing the feet of commoners—including the very one who would betray Him—and ultimately allowing callous others to kill Him. The Creator-God was willing to die as my Redeemer-Friend! The very least I can do is treat my fellow slaves of Jesus with this kind of humility; yet the Master asks more, even my very best, humbly serving *everyone* this way!

Slaves of Jesus experience the destruction of the competitive spirit within them, as they realize they are no better—nor less!—than any other slave of the Master. We find personal satisfaction in following His example to humbly serve others. At the same time, we may receive appreciation from people as we serve our family, our neighbors and our bosses as unto the Lord (see Col. 3:22-23). But instead of seeking how high we can go in the stations of this world, we seek how humbly we can serve, thinking little of ourselves and much of the Master. His path to blessing is different: "God sets himself against the proud but he shows favor to the humble" (Jas. 4:6).

Our Master models the role He would have His slaves follow in serving others.

> *Remember that the Lord will give you an inheritance as your reward, and the Master you are serving is Christ. . . . Store your treasures in heaven, where they will never become moth-eaten or rusty and where they will be safe from thieves. . . . How we praise God, the Father of our Lord Jesus Christ, who has blessed us with every spiritual blessing in the heavenly realms because we belong to Christ (Col. 3:24; Matt. 6:20; Eph. 1:3).*

Does humility characterize my life?

When we focus on the things of this world, we are ignoring the treasures we have in Christ. Our Lord Jesus said to think first of Him and seek first His kingdom, and all these "things" shall be added unto you (see Matt. 6:33)!

Think of it! We have the greatest news ever announced. We know the greatest Person who ever lived. We have access to all that He has, and that's no small sum (like unto "the cattle on a thousand hills"). We are rich! And yet we act like the old Texan, Mr. Yates, on his sheep ranch—downtrodden, apparently impoverished, a person without a clue to the billions of barrels of oil beneath the ground he walked upon. The potential blessing of an abundant oil field was his, but he was totally unaware until an oil company struck the largest pool of oil ever found up until that time. He was land-poor until he, with others, looked in the right places. Where is the eye of our faith looking?

"And this same God who takes care of me will supply all your needs from his glorious riches, which have been given to us in Christ Jesus" (Phil. 4:19). It all comes together in Him, and it is all wrapped up in Him, and He is ours and we are His. Think of the treasures we can access: The secrets of God! The mercies of God! The pleasure and approval of God! And much, much more, all of it found in Christ! This is no lottery, no product of random chance. This was designed by the Master Architect of the universe, and it is all for you and me! Are we keeping this glorious news to ourselves?

This wealth we have in Christ is not only for the by and by; it is for the now and now. "We have this treasure in earthen vessels," Paul said (2 Cor. 4:7, *NASB*). Never was this marvel made more clear to me than the way God responded to the terminal illness He permitted in my life. I was seen by the nation's top lung specialists in two reputed clinics, but, to be blunt, I was sent home to die, expecting about 90 days to live. But soon after arriving back in Orlando in the early spring of 2001, dear friends, Pearl and Jack Galpin, introduced me to a Russian scientist and physician who specialized in lung disease.

A coincidence? Not one bit! This was a total God-incident in response to the prayers of countless friends and to the faith decision Vonette and I made to thank the Lord and praise Him in spite of the disease. The physician, Dr. Svetlana Ivanova, holds degrees in philosophy and medicine. She was a research scientist and for six years worked at Chernobyl in charge of pulmonary diseases. She had come as an immigrant to America and was befriended by the Galpins who insisted that I see her. Because she was an immigrant with no work permit and no U.S. medical license, she was able to give her full attention to my condition! (God's timing is so exquisite!) For 30 consecutive days, three times per day, she treated me in a tent with special aroma oils. If she had been in Russia in full practice, I would have been 1 of 100. Instead, I was her only patient! Then, she reduced the frequency of the treatments and, slowly, my lungs developed an *increased* capacity to breathe over what I had been experiencing for the previous year! My life was extended from one to two years because God sent her to help me.

═══

Our Master shares His supernatural riches with His slaves.

> *This letter is from Paul, Jesus Christ's slave, chosen by God to be an apostle and sent out to preach his Good News. . . . If others have reason for confidence in their own efforts, I have even more! . . . I once thought all these things were so very important, but now I consider them worthless because of what Christ has done. Yes, everything else is worthless when compared with the priceless gain of knowing Christ Jesus my Lord. I have discarded everything else, counting it all as garbage, so that I may have Christ and become one with Him (Rom. 1:1; Phil. 3:4,7-9).*

Am I experiencing the reality of His supernatural resources?

═══

Although I still had to be on oxygen regularly, I was praising God for that Russian scientist who became a beloved friend. One morning, God seemed to remind me: "Bill, you sowed your entire retirement account in faith to open a New Life Training Center at Moscow State University back in 1990, when the Soviet Union crumbled. You had prayed for Russia since 1947. Your seed of faith sown in Russia is growing up as health for you in America through the life of an obedient Russian!"

To God be all the glory! Please know that I am telling this account merely to illustrate what God does as we honor Him in obedience and faith. We are rich in whatever we sow in faith with God!

Recognition from the world system has its appeal to the ego. We are taught as children to constantly strive to climb a ladder of success, to attain diplomas, degrees and job promotions and titles. It is not that these are unworthy tools; it is just that praise from the world system is a flickering candle compared to the flame of the personal knowledge of Christ and His Spirit, His Word and His way. The world's praise can often be fickle and superficial. For example, the masses hailed Jesus as King on Sunday and crucified Him on Friday!

Our Master calls us to seek first His kingdom.

> *He who is a hired hand, and not a shepherd, who is not the owner of the sheep, sees the wolf coming, and leaves the sheep and flees, and the wolf snatches them and scatters them. He flees because he is a hired hand and is not concerned about the sheep (John 10:12-13, NASB).*

Whose kingdom am I serving?

Paul, after he had met our Lord Jesus on the road to Damascus, turned his back on all the prideful accomplishment he had as a scholar, as a "Hebrew of Hebrews." He discounted his royal bloodlines, religious zeal, the approval of men and even the highest scholars and religious leaders of his times. Not until Paul was turned away from all that human attention did he become a slave of Jesus. Then, he became an apostle, and he helped change the world forever.

Our Master expects His slaves to think and serve by His royal standards.

When you obey me, you remain in my love, just as I obey my Father and remain in his love. I have told you this so that you will be filled with my joy. Yes, your joy will overflow! (John 15:10-12).

Am I joyfully serving the Lord Jesus with excellence?

Slaves of Jesus know who is the real source of any earthly achievements and give any glory or credit entirely to the Lord. It has been my privilege to receive an abundance of recognitions by my peers—eight honorary degrees, the $1 million global Templeton Prize for Progress in Religion, numerous awards from the Christian and official leadership community in America and in other lands. I appreciate these awards and value the good fellowship and opportunity these provide for me to say from my heart: "All glory goes to the Lord, our great Creator-God and Savior." But they all pale in comparison to one moment of ecstasy with our Lord while reading His Word, while hearing His Spirit speak, while enjoying the fullness of His presence. Slaves of Jesus know whose reward really counts, and they walk in that knowledge joyfully. They know to put all problems and all praise on the altar—to kneel, thank God and walk away. Credentials, plaques and awards are fine and often necessary for wider ministry; but trusting in them or flaunting them is not becoming of a slave of Jesus.

Hired workers come and go. They punch the clock and do not risk themselves for the mission of the Master. Having made no life commitment, they never become part of the family household.

Slaves by choice, on the other hand, stay on duty even when legally freed. They choose to stay under the authority and commands of their Master. To understand the concept fully, we must distinguish a bondservant (Greek *doulos*), who was a slave, from a hired servant (Greek *diakonos*), who was not a slave. To some degree, this is a parallel between the life of a Spirit-filled Christian and the carnal, worldly Christian. Spirit-filled Christians serve without hesitation because they love the Master who first loved them. Carnal Christians serve out of a sense of duty, for recognition and reward, or in fear of punishment.

Slaves of Jesus know that their royal service has excellence for its operating standard. The joys of not settling for second-best are worth occasional delays and disappointments. Mediocrity is not even an option for slaves of Jesus. To know, love, trust and obey Jesus is to seek His perfect will, His excellence and His glory in all things. Being a slave of Jesus never means spiritual poverty. It means obeying the Excellent One wherever He sends, whatever He asks, to the very best of our ability and having faith in the enabling power of His Spirit.

> Don't you realize that whatever you choose to obey becomes your master? You can choose sin, which leads to death, or you can choose to obey God and receive his approval. . . . But now you are free from the power of sin and have become slaves of God. Now you do those things that lead to holiness and result in eternal life. . . . Anyone who isn't helping me opposes me, and anyone who isn't working with me is actually working against me (Rom. 6:16,22; Luke 11:23).

Compromise kills the effective witness of any follower of Christ. The joy of belonging to Jesus obviously has a corollary: We do not belong to the world system. There is a line drawn in the sands of time. On one side are those holy and separated unto God; on the other side is everyone else. "Who is on the Lord's side?" the prophet asked. We have been chosen, but we must accept the separation from sin and worldly behavior that comes with His selection of us.

A THOUGHT FROM VONETTE

Early in our ministry, my husband developed a simple way of sharing his faith in Christ with others. He called it "God's Plan," and it included spiritual "laws" or steps for finding God's grace. Eventually, this plan became The Four Spiritual Laws, a booklet Christians can use to tell others about the Good News of Jesus Christ. Each of the staff members of Campus Crusade would memorize the presentation.

One morning, at 2:00 a.m., several women and I were in a downstairs room of our home typing a draft of "God's Plan" to be used for a presentation for the following day. Bill had gone to bed because he faced a full schedule in the morning.

Suddenly, he came running down the stairs, telling us that the first law had to be rewritten. Originally, the first law explained that people are sinful and need to repent before they can have a relationship with God. At that time, the approach was common in Christian circles. But Bill wanted to begin with an emphasis on God's love, because he felt this is what draws people to God. In fact, he believed that God's love is the foremost principle of the universe. So the first law became "God loves you and has a wonderful plan for your life."

This law was not only true for the moment when you came to Christ and were forgiven of all your sins, but it is also the foundation for your Christian life. That's what makes our spiritual journey such an adventure of joy.

Sometimes, I see Christians confused about being "set apart" from the world because of the struggle with sin in their lives. I have come to believe it is because they do not realize all that Jesus accomplished in and for them at the cross. They do not realize the greatness of our justification (we have been declared "just as if we had never sinned.") When they first come to Him by *faith* for salvation, they are to continue by faith in being sanctified (see Col. 2:6). Our sanctification has been illustrated this way: We are saved sinners in a boat on the lake of life; we are to stir the waters and bring positive change, but we are not to let the water in the boat!

"Stop loving this evil world and all that it offers you, for when you love the world, you show that you do not have the love of the Father in you" (1 John 2:15). Just as any water must be bailed out of a boat, lest it sink, so also we must immediately confess any sin that enters our life (see Ps. 66:18; 1 John 1:9). Here is a further illustration: Some find it amusing when I reply to certain requests with: "Well, I am not sure about that; you will have to take it up with Vonette's husband." My point is, I chose her and SHE chose me; I am the only one of my kind, set apart for her and her alone. I am hers and she has rights and claims on me, my time and my talent. I cannot get mixed up in any activities that are not clearly of Vonette's choosing. This is an expression of obedience to God's command for me to love Vonette sacrificially as Christ loves the Church and died for it. How much more is this so with the Lord to whom I literally and completely belong!

Slaves of Jesus know that in God's eyes they now belong to Him, and His love sees *not their* sin but the sacrifice of the Savior who died for our sins; so we are clean and in perfect standing with Him. It is as if we stand naked before God and He finds not one imperfection of any kind! We are even the right weight!

All of this adds up to one of the most amazing and exhilarating truths of all time for me. Despite our acts of sin, despite our depraved sinful nature, when we received Him as Lord and Savior, He wrote across our souls: "Blameless!" (see Eph. 1:4). Is that the greatest news ever announced? Yes! It opens the door for us into the Holy of Holies: We can go to God directly and express our praise, our needs, our failures; and He hears our heart and reminds us: "Blameless!" Not a blot nor blemish on our record! We are as a criminal whose history has been expunged by the Judge of Eternity. It is like children playing and getting very soiled from dirt and grass stains, but their mother scrubs them up and by the time the father gets home, the children stand before him squeaky clean and shining with smiles! This is a picture of the position of believers in Christ. Hallelujah, what a Savior!

Our Master expects His slaves to serve with integrity.

For such men are slaves, not of our Lord Christ but of their own appetites; and by their smooth and flattering speech they deceive the hearts of the unsuspecting (Rom. 16:18, NASB).

Am I a person of integrity?

How do we succeed? Not by any means possible! The world often approves of greed, guilt and guile as motives. And, if I cooperate with the world system, I find myself hungry for attention and approval of others. I am not happy until my desire for recognition is quenched, and then only for a little while. As a result, I might become willing to say or do things to trick others into saying or doing things I want to hear or experience. This is the cancer of manipulation. But there is a healthier way to live: I can choose the honest and direct ways of my Master.

"Most of all, my brothers and sisters, never take an oath, by heaven or earth or anything else. Just say a simple yes or no, so that you will not sin and be condemned for it" (Jas. 5:12). I can decide to hunger only for His approval rather than the flattery of men. "Obviously, I'm not trying to be a people pleaser! No, I am trying to please God. If I were still trying to please people, I would not be Christ's servant" (Gal. 1:10). I can decide to be satisfied with His appraisal of me no matter what others may say. As a result, I want to keep my words and deeds in harmony with His will for my life.

Slaves of Jesus talk straight. As a result, they do not have to keep mental lists of untruths they must try to cover up. They know the certainty of the adage: "Oh, the tangled web we weave when first we practice to deceive." Tragically, the terrible cost of lies and cover-ups is played out before the world by elected officials, corporate executives, professional athletes and, yes, men in the pulpit. By contrast, slaves of Jesus know that truth and obedience are their best allies in the struggles of this world. Truth is the sure way to release God's power in our lives. We are freed at last from the vain deceptions of the world system when we face the truth and tell the truth! And it is the Lord Jesus Himself who said, "I am . . . the truth" (John 14:6). When we let Him live His life through us, we are governed by truth. The blessed irony is that as we live this way, the world often respects such behavior, and we will very likely find favor with God and man.

The Master always keeps His word and expects His slaves to do the same.

> *Understand, therefore, that the LORD your God is indeed God. He is the faithful God who keeps his covenant for a thousand generations and constantly loves those who love him and obey his commands (Deut. 7:9-10).*

Is there anything I value more highly than being trusted by Jesus?

The high standards to which we are called can seem overwhelming. In fact, they are impossible in our own strength. But let us celebrate what God's Word says: "God, who calls you, is faithful; he will do this" (1 Thess. 5:24). He cannot deny His promises. He will not lie. Paul adds, "And I am sure that God, who began the good work within you, will continue his work until it is finally finished on that day when Christ Jesus comes back again" (Phil. 1:6).

His life in us enables a yielded believer to be effective without resorting to selfish and evil schemes.

True Humility

His Choice

Once we adopt the correct attitude toward God, it is much easier to have the right attitude about ourselves. But one problem we have is allowing ourselves to get in the way of our calling as a slave for Jesus. After reading the following verses, explain the position of a slave.

Matthew 16:24

_____
_____
_____
_____

Galatians 2:20

_____
_____
_____
_____

John 13:13-17

_____
_____
_____

My Choice

Now that you have examined your position as a slave for Jesus, write how you will accomplish this goal in your life. For each point, make your comments specific to your daily activities so that you can begin to apply each of the positions above.

Avoid materialism (Luke 16:13; 1 Tim. 6:10).

_____

_____

_____

_____

Adopt the humility of Jesus (Col. 3:22-23).

_____

_____

_____

_____

Depend on God's supernatural riches (Phil. 4:19).

_____

_____

_____

_____

Seek God's kingdom first (Phil. 3:7-10).

_____

_____

_____

_____

Guard against compromise (Rom. 6:16-17).

_____

_____

_____

_____

Be dependable (Phil. 1:9-11).

_____

_____

_____

5

SHARING WHAT WE KNOW

Choice Point
Take the initiative to introduce others to your Master.

Slaves of Jesus are either serving or they are ill! Even then, they can pray for the needs of others! The essence of their lives is to project the love of the Lord to others. One cannot merely think wonderful thoughts in solitude; one must take the truth of God's Word to others. Here are some of the ways that slaves of Jesus interact with others:

> But when the Holy Spirit has come upon you, you will re-
> ceive power to testify about Me with great effect, to the
> people in Jerusalem, throughout Judea, in Samaria, and
> to the ends of the earth, about my death and resurrection
> (Acts 1:8, *TLB*).

When we began the ministry of Campus Crusade for Christ on the campus of the University of California in Los Angeles, in 1951, a student named Joe quickly caught my attention. Now, Joe didn't stand out for the usual reasons we associate with college students. He was no "brain," nor was he handsome. He was no athlete, not a sharp dresser, and neither did he drive a fancy car. He did not have an engaging personality, and he was not wealthy. So why, you surely wonder, did Joe stand out in the crowd?

Joe stood out in the crowd for one reason: He probably introduced more students to Jesus Christ during his years at UCLA than all the other Christians combined. He loved Jesus and had a zeal for telling others about Him. Joe would report to me regularly, telling about students he had introduced to Christ, and we would rejoice together. I remember Joe today as a truly remarkable young man.

During those days at UCLA, a friend made an offhand comment about Joe: "If Joe didn't have the Lord, he wouldn't have anything, would he?" I had to agree with him, but it made me realize that my friend's statement was not just true about Joe; it was true about me and about all of us! What, where or who would any of us be if it were not for Jesus? Think about the original bunch of scruffy characters Jesus called out of the backwaters of Galilee to be His disciples. Who were they? Today we would call them blue-collar workers; just regular guys. I have a feeling that if Jesus had walked on the campus of UCLA to pick a band of followers, Joe would have been one of the twelve.

Joe epitomized what Jesus called His disciple-slaves to be: "One day as Jesus was walking along the shores of the Sea of Galilee, he saw Simon and his brother, Andrew, fishing with a net, for they were commercial fishermen. Jesus called out to them, 'Come, be my disciples, and I will show you how to fish for people!' At once they left their nets and went with him" (Mark 1:16-18). Joe was a fisher of men. Sometimes the person who does what is normal stands out in a crowd because no one else is doing anything. Something that should be ordinary takes on the appearance of being extraordinary because it is seen so infrequently. Every Christian, as a normal course of events, should be introducing others to the Lord Jesus, as a way of life.

There are two main reasons why slaves of Christ are fishers of men. The first reason is because our Master has commanded it. A form of the Great Commission—His command for us to go and disciple the nations—is found in all four gospels (see Matt. 28:18-20; Mark 16:15-18; Luke 24:45-49; John 20:21-23). This command Jesus summarized just before His ascension into heaven in Acts 1:8. We are commanded to be His witnesses. For us not to introduce others to Christ is a major act of disobedience; a crack in the foundational characteristic of the master-slave relationship.

He came to seek and to save the lost, and He commanded us to finish what He came to the world to do—seek and save the lost.

The second reason we should tell others about Jesus is because of who He is and what He has done for us—and for all people. I am always amazed to meet Christians who give glowing testimonies about who Christ is and what He means to them, but they never talk about introducing others to Him. Why would we not want everyone to know about the Lord and Savior who has done for us what no one else has ever done? He loved us. He died for us. He rose from the dead and now lives within us. Oh, how wonderful is our Savior! Everyone needs Him.

Our Master is pleased when His slaves speak of Him to others.

> *Epaphras, from your city, a servant [doulos] of Christ Jesus, sends you his greetings. He always prays earnestly for you, asking God to make you strong and perfect, fully confident of the whole will of God (Col. 4:12).*

How many people have I introduced to Jesus?

What a reputation Epaphras had! His name means *lovely*. He was known to be a prayer warrior, and as a result, his name is listed among the early believers upon whose lives the Lord built the church. He had the spirit of Samuel, who led by example: "God forbid that I should sin against the LORD in ceasing to pray for you" (1 Sam. 12:23, *KJV*).

As a slave of Jesus, Epaphras was not self-centered. He cared about his fellow sojourners. He had prayer goals in mind for them—for their spiritual maturity, their confidence in God and His Word, and their resting in the purpose and plan of God for their lives.

Epaphras worked at prayer, which is the first labor of love. We are to "pray without ceasing" (1 Thess. 5:17, *NASB*). Rather than having our minds wander about worldly ideas, we obey the Master's request to work at prayer for others. Our Lord Jesus, as He finished the dark hours of Gethsemane, asked the disciples, "Couldn't you stay awake and watch with me even one hour?" (Matt. 26:40). When we pray, we also are saying no to various voices that appeal to the ego or draw us away from simple service and toward vainglory, which is the applause of this world's recognition and reward system. Interceding for others is not particularly easy, but the Master did not say to pray when we *feel* like it; He said to pray!

Our Master will answer whatever He impresses His slaves to pray for.

Whoever wants to be first must be the slave of all. . . . If any man serve me, him will My Father honor. . . . When you bow down before the Lord and admit your dependence on him, he will lift you up and give you honor (Mark 10:44; John 12:26, KJV; Jas. 4:10).

Do I believe the promise of Philippians 2:13: "For God is working in you, giving you the desire to obey him and the power to do what pleases him"?

Slaves of Jesus enjoy living with a Master who knows each of us by our very own name, and so does the circle of influence and fellowship surrounding us. As we pray, it is satisfying to know that we are being obedient in what the Master asked. It also is a great reward to see others grow in their maturity. We may be surprised to meet people for the first time who celebrate how God used something we said or prayed or wrote as having positive impact in their lives. They say, "I feel like I know you." That's because, in Christ, we are known members of the Royal Household, having the same Master, and we may often meet at the throne room of prayer!

The Lord Jesus inverts the recognition ladder. My attitude is to be that of a simple slave. He frees me and inspires me to serve others gladly. There are no corporate ladders to climb, no Grammy or Golden Globes to grab. Instead of striving for recognition for myself, I serve those whom the Master loves. I choose this approach to life not as drudgery but as delight. Though I have been blessed with many honors on this earth, for which I am grateful, nevertheless they were by-products of my heart's goal: to hear the Master say, "Well done!"

Slaves of Jesus have clarified motives for what we do. We can relax to be our authentic, newborn selves as we obey Him. We are freed from anxiously striving, even as we physically work hard. Personal ambition and the competitive spirit are shackled; we are no longer driven by the need for approval of anyone but our Master. We are freed from the scorekeeping and recognition devices of this world's system. By virtue of serving others humbly, we are recognized and ranked by God Himself! We gain honor from *Him*!

Our Master honors those who serve Him and His kingdom.

> *So why do you condemn another Christian? Why do you look down on another Christian? . . . Who are you to condemn God's servants? They are responsible to the Lord, so let Him tell them whether they are right or wrong (Rom. 14:10,4).*

What motivates me to serve others?

Each day we are faced with the decision of whether to sit in judgment of each other. In nearly six decades of walking with our Lord, I cannot describe the damage done to the cause of Christ by Christians judging Christians in public and private. This ought not to be so. We are disobedient to our Master when we decide to judge another. He instructed us on how to deal with those we feel have grieved us (see Matt. 18:15-17). He told us to "judge not, and you will not be judged; condemn not, and you will not be condemned; forgive, and you will be forgiven" (Luke 6:37, *ESV*). He warned us, "The disciple is not above his master: but every one that is perfect shall be as his master" (John 15:20, *KJV*).

> And why worry about a speck in your friend's eye when you have a log in your own? How can you think of saying, "Friend, let me help you get rid of that speck in your eye," when you can't see past the log in your own eye? Hypocrite! First get rid of the log from your own eye; then perhaps you will see well enough to deal with the speck in your friend's eye (Luke 6:41-42).

Our Master expects His slaves to love, not judge, one another.

Lord, take note of their threats, and grant that Your bond-servants may speak Your word with all confidence. . . . Now you are free from the power of sin and have become slaves of God. Now you do those things that lead to holiness and result in eternal life (Acts 4:29, NASB; Rom. 6:22).

Am I known for judging or for loving?

In the small community where I grew up, gossip was an avocation—perhaps not much different from the chatter in big-city office and apartment complexes. My saintly mother taught us children that we were no better than anyone else and nobody was better than we were. Putting other people down can be one way some folks get through the day, trying to make themselves feel superior. But in my community, I noticed that the best ranchers and business leaders talked about their own duties and very little about the dirt of others. If they did learn of a neighbor's problem, they went straight to that person to offer help, not to pry. Similarly, the Lord Jesus simplifies my life for me. He wants me to stay focused on my accountability to Him and avoid condemning others. By doing so, I show faith in His promise to deal with me fairly and defend me in the face of opposition.

Our Master expects His slaves to be "salt and light" for Him in society.

> *You are the salt of the earth. But what good is salt if it has lost its flavor? Can you make it useful again? It will be thrown out and trampled underfoot as worthless. You are the light of the world—like a city on a mountain, glowing in the night for all to see. Don't hide your light under a basket! Instead, put it on a stand and let it shine for all. In the same way, let your good deeds shine out for all to see, so that everyone will praise your heavenly Father (Matt. 5:13-16).*

How is the world different because of my presence?

Slaves of Jesus cast their fate into the Master's keeping. Rather than looking on the work of others with a critical spirit, we keep our eyes on our God-given assignments. In so doing, we may feel vulnerable to the criticism of others. But God is constantly seeking to "protect our back" as we move forward in faith following Him. The "armor of God" has no back armor because (1) we are to always be moving forward, and (2) covering that side is the Master's responsibility! We can fight the good fight more freely because we are not sitting in judgment of others. We concentrate on being totally ready to stand before Him with a clean heart and a clear conscience.

A THOUGHT FROM VONETTE

Through our service to others, God wants us to influence our world for Him. But when we look at our circumstances and the society in which we live, we may feel overwhelmed and consider our inclusion insignificant.

Many of the prophets of the Old Testament and the disciples in the New Testament felt much the same way. When God called Moses to lead the people out of Egypt, Moses argued, "Oh, Lord, I'm just not a good speaker. I have never been, and I'm not now, even after you have spoken to me. I'm clumsy with words" (Exod. 4:10). In Exodus 4:14, we are told that God was displeased with Moses' response. God is also displeased with our excuses. When God gives us a task, we may be tempted to say, "I don't have the ability" or "Someone else is much more capable." My dear Bill knew that there were other men much more capable than he; however, his totally surrendered life gave him great strength.

Shall we be the "salt and light" our Lord commanded in the Sermon on the Mount? Or shall we let the world intimidate us into silence due to a false, fear-based "modesty"? The Lord Jesus gives me boldness in the face of fear, to speak His word despite threats and dangers. If I had to do this all by myself, well, I probably would not do it. But as I choose to submit myself to the Master, I can see all kinds of miracles take place. I choose to collaborate with the Master who has set the example for me, and He has commanded me to go in His name: "When the Holy Spirit has come upon you, you will receive power and will tell people about me everywhere—in Jerusalem, throughout Judea, in Samaria, and to the ends of the earth" (Acts 1:8).

Slaves of Jesus have strength to do their duties, and boldness to proclaim the words of the Master in the face of opposition. Our strongest and most undeniable witness is how we love each other. We enjoy access to life-changing, society-transforming power in the mighty name of Jesus!

Our Master sacrificed His life for everyone, not just His slaves.

"As the Father has sent me, so send I you. . . ." *For though I am free from all men, I have made myself a slave to all, so that I may win more. . . . So everywhere we go, we tell everyone about Christ. We warn them and teach them with all the wisdom God has given us, for we want to present them to God, perfect in their relationship to Christ (John 20:21, NASB; 1 Cor. 9:19, NASB; Col. 1:28).*

Do I love others without regard to race or economic class?

The Lord Jesus looks on the heart—not skin, race, gender, tribal roots, economic status or religiosity. God had plans for the people of Israel who rejected Him, but He made it a point to open wide the doors of His kingdom to all. I cannot sit by and pick and choose to share His invitation only with those I personally prefer. How can I be in good standing with Him if I have malice in my heart toward any person or group of persons for whom He died?

Slaves of Jesus make sure that the "most joyful news ever announced" is available to one and all. What are we doing with our lives this very day to accomplish that goal? Are we wasting precious opportunities to tell others? No, an assignment is constantly pending: Go to all and compel them. God wants a kingdom populated with those who love the Master.

Jesus came to seek and save the lost (see Luke 19:10). He commands all of us, His followers, to complete the assignment He gave us, to help fulfill the Great Commission (see Matt. 28:18-20).

Do I really want to follow the Lord, to serve as He did? How can I serve that way while bound up in my own little world, focusing only on my problems? The Lord Jesus frees me to become "enslaved" to others, to win them. This is an attitude I can choose to have in the midst of daily struggles. I must never forget what life is all about—reaching others with the love of God shown by the Master, who came into this world "to seek and to save that which was lost" (Luke 19:10, *NASB*) and who commissions me to follow Him on that mission.

Our Master expects His slaves to help fulfill the Great Commission.

A slave [is not] above His master. . . . You must make allowance for each other's faults and forgive the person who offends you. Remember, the Lord forgave you, so you must forgive others (Matt. 10:24, NASB; Col. 3:13).

What is my personal strategy for obeying the Great Commission?

Slaves of Jesus know this secret about the liberty in slavery: Our freedom comes as we freely follow His command to help fulfill the Great Commission. Our Master lets us strategize with Him to find new ways to effectively communicate the gospel. His message does not change, but the methods and means do as we follow His example in reaching all persons of all walks of life, everywhere, from my neighborhood to the villages and capitals of every region of the earth.

Jesus says, "Follow Me, and I will make you fishers of men" (Matt. 4:19, *NASB*). If we are not fishing, we are not following.

I doubt there is a sweeter word in any language than "forgiven"! It falls joyously on the ear of a sinner like me; a criminal convicted in the court of God's justice; a debtor with no income or accounts; a traveler with no means, no destination, no destiny. But in Christ we are forgiven! Any way you look at it, being forgiven gives new zest for living, makes life an adventure, provides purpose and destiny, leads to heaven as our home! And how many times have we been forgiven? Thank You, Lord, for paying for every single penalty I have earned and every debt to You I could never repay!

How can we respond to such love and forgiveness? Here are two ways: First, the only way we can even approach God about the joy of being forgiven and belonging to Him is to say, "Thank You, Lord Jesus!" We dare not be as the ungrateful lepers who went merrily on their way, healed of a physical sickness but still suffering from heart trouble! Only one returned to say, "Thank You!" (see Luke 17:11-19). Second, we can obey Him when He said to forgive others. Slaves of Jesus are taught to pray, "Forgive us our sins, just as we have forgiven those who have sinned against us" (Matt. 6:12). Paul said to the Ephesians, "[Forgive] one another, just as God through Christ has forgiven you" (Eph. 4:32). The apostle Peter once asked Jesus how many times we should forgive—seven times? Our Lord replied, "Seventy times seven!" (see Matt. 18:21-22). But some people seem to push the limit, don't they? Are you up to about 489 "forgivens" with someone? Forgive again and keep on forgiving as many times as God has forgiven you!

For example, when I break fellowship with Vonette, I can sense it immediately. I do not want to be in that condition for a minute if at all possible. Quickly and sincerely, I say, "I was wrong. I am sorry. Please forgive me. I love you." Through the years, she has learned by my actions as well that I dearly mean every word. And then I hear her say, "Forgiven!" The most beautiful response one can give! It is like getting married again! I love her and she loves me, and I am forgiven! Let's go celebrate!

Slaves of Jesus know that as we receive the good news of forgiveness, and share it and practice it, the world will never be the same, and all glory will go to the only one deserving of credit—our matchless Lord and Savior, Creator and Redeemer, the Great Forgiver of the fallen! "Oh the love that drew salvation's plan; Oh the grace that brought it down to man. Oh the mighty gulf that God did span at Calvary."[1] Get up, my weary friend, you are forgiven! If only a small percentage of believers actually live this way, it will fuel a global revolution.

Our Master expects His slaves to always forgive others.

> *If you forgive those who sin against you, your heavenly Father will forgive you. But if you refuse to forgive others, your Father will not forgive your sins (Matt. 6:14-15).*

Is there anyone in my life whom I have not forgiven?

Sharing What We Know

Attitudes mean everything. Sometimes we can hide our attitudes from others and even from ourselves. But we can't hide them or our motives from God. While you answer the following questions, take some time to ask God to reveal your attitudes toward others.

His Choice

Read Acts 1:8. How did the story about Joe, a student on the UCLA campus, illustrate this command from Jesus?

_____

_____

_____

_____

_____

What is the attitude of a slave toward others (see 1 Cor. 9:19-23)?

_____

_____

_____

_____

_____

_____

The definition for witnessing to others about Jesus is: *Success in witnessing is simply taking the initiative to share Christ in the power of the Holy Spirit and leaving the results to God.* What does this mean to you?

_____

_____

_____

_____

_____

How should we tell about Jesus (see Luke 14:16-23).

_____

_____

_____

_____

_____

_____

My Choice

In the following sets of verses, you will find ways to serve others. Write each way and how you will incorporate this into your everyday life.

Colossians 4:12

_____

_____

_____

_____

Romans 14:4,10

_____
_____
_____
_____
_____
_____

Matthew 5:13-16

_____
_____
_____
_____
_____

Colossians 3:13; Ephesians 4:32

_____
_____
_____
_____
_____

Note
1. William R. Newell (1868–1956), "At Calvary."

6

TRUE ABUNDANT LIVING

Choice Point
Forgive much because you have been forgiven much more.

As we ponder daily realities, including the awesomeness of God and our place in His great plan, we soon develop certain attitudes about the journey called life. *Attitude determines altitude,* says a popular leadership slogan. This is much like Paul's admonition: "Since you have been raised to new life with Christ, set your sights on the realities of heaven, where Christ sits at God's right hand in the place of honor and power. Let heaven fill your thoughts. Do not think only about things down here on earth" (Col. 3:1-2). One paraphrase records, "You should have as little desire for this world as a dead man does" (*TLB*).

Paul sharpens the matter of our focus in Philippians 4:8: "Fix your thoughts on what is true and honorable and right. Think about things that are pure and lovely and admirable. Think about things that are excellent and worthy of praise." As I have observed slaves of Jesus across this planet, I have seen some of these attitudes toward life that seem to dominate their view of joyful living:

If you keep yourself pure, you will be a utensil God can use for his purpose. Your life will be clean, and you will be ready for the Master to use you for every good work.... But I am afraid that, as the serpent deceived Eve by his craftiness, your minds will be led astray from the

simplicity and purity of devotion to Christ (2 Tim. 2:21;
2 Cor. 11:3, *NASB*).

The Christian life is so simple that many misunderstand it
and, as a result, fail to enjoy it. But God made it so that anyone, in
any language, with childlike faith, can know Him and experience
His salvation and abundant living. I have found that all of life's
challenges can be faced in victory as we, with the radiance of a
royal slave, love, trust and obey our great Creator-God and Savior,
the Master of all. He wants us to keep our relationship pure from
sin and the world, and He wants our lives in Him kept simple—all
accounts promptly settled, all assignments understood and car-
ried out. He wants us to be always leaning forward in faith for
what He has for us! Certainly, our relationship with God can be
seen as very complex. But I am convinced that adopting the attitudes of a royal slave of Christ is the way to live simply and fruit-
fully, no matter the world situation or my personal circumstances.

**Our Master simplifies the roles of His slaves for fruitful and abun-
dant living.**

> *Remember the word that I said to you, "A slave is not greater
> than his master." If they persecuted Me, they will also persecute
> you. . . . Here on earth you will have many trials and sorrows.
> But take heart, because I have overcome the world (John 15:20,
> NASB; 16:33).*

Are the purposes of Jesus being accomplished through my life?

Slaves of Jesus have so many reasons for keeping a close relationship with their Lord—from salvation to security to sanctification to heaven itself, and blessings along the way! They know

that the job of a slave is to ask, *Am I obeying the Master, yielded and controlled by His Holy Spirit, or am I trying to solve problems in my own strength?* Keep life pure and simple! Say yes where Jesus did and no where He did! Very practical issues are resolved by the simplicity of the mindset of one who belongs to Jesus. Take the challenge of frustration, for example. A slave of Jesus obeys and leaves the results to the Master. If all of today's work is not getting done today, the Master knows the situation and He can teach us better time management, He can rearrange other people's schedules to make it all work out, or He can show us that the assignment belongs to someone else. Perhaps He will enable us to work smarter and faster, especially as we talk with Him about the matter!

The Lord Jesus warns me of coming dangers, especially conflicts with those in our culture who despise Him. In fact, He says my service will be similar to His own, and that means persecution, often from the religious elite! It also means expecting to overcome all the difficulties life can bring.

A THOUGHT FROM VONETTE

We decided to accept Bill's illness as a new adventure in trusting God to meet our needs. He always had met our needs, and I really believed that God would heal Bill. God does not promise that only good things will happen to His children. But He does promise that whatever happens He will use for our eternal benefit. We may not always understand the reason for difficulties in our life, but God can and will use bad things to make us better.

When the physician announced that I had a terminal illness, Vonette and I, by faith, began praising the Lord and thanking Him in simple obedience. The Bible says, "Always be joyful. Keep on praying. No matter what happens, always be thankful, for this is God's will for you who belong to Christ Jesus" (1 Thess. 5:16-18). We also had His Word of understanding: "We can rejoice, too, when we run into problems and trials, for we know that they are good for us—they help us learn to endure. And endurance develops strength of character in us, and character strengthens our confident expectation of salvation" (Rom. 5:3-4). We understood the way God works: "Whenever trouble comes your way, let it be an opportunity for joy. For when your faith is tested, your endurance has a chance to grow. So let it grow, for when your endurance is fully developed, you will be strong in character and ready for anything" (Jas. 1:2-4).

Since the doctor announced I was dying, the Lord has enabled me to write as never before, to videotape more than 350 hours of teaching and to help launch a network for pastors, which is designed to help launch 5 million house churches during the next 10 years and help turn millions of those who make decisions for Christ into disciples.

Our Master requires His slaves to cast all their cares on Him.

> *Once a religious leader asked Jesus this question: "Good teacher, what should I do to get eternal life? . . . I've obeyed all these commandments since I was a child." . . . "There is still one thing you lack," Jesus said. "Sell all you have and give the money to the poor, and you will have treasure in heaven. Then come, follow me." But when the man heard this, he became sad because he was very rich. Jesus watched him go and then said to his disciples, "How hard it is for rich people to get into the Kingdom of God!" (Luke 18:18,21-24).*

Am I obeying my Lord by putting everything under His sovereign control?

Slaves of Jesus know that He was persecuted and crucified for obeying the will of God for His life. He candidly forewarned us to expect no less. The Early Church *expected* to die for their beliefs yet lived in joy and praise! How? This victory is not in a formula but in a Person, the Master who has conquered whatever difficulties we may face. He has overcome any problem we may face (see Heb. 4:14-16). Knowing this makes it easier to follow the Master. He advises us in advance how to depend on Him in trials, tests and temptations. And His confiding in us builds our confidence in Him and in ourselves.

We are merely pilgrims on a journey through time. Everything we may hold in our hands belongs to the Lord Jesus. As a result, I have a completely different attitude about the possessions in my life. First, I must take great care of what are truly *His* possessions—and that includes me! I am a temple of His Holy Spirit (see 1 Cor. 6:19-20)! Second, the things that the world may consider as mine actually belong to Him. So, if someone steals or abuses this property, that person has a problem with the Master, not me. It is not my place to seek revenge; the Master will bring justice to the situation, in time or eternity. It all belongs to Him.

Once, I had a partner in an oil-drilling project in Pauls Valley, Oklahoma. My partner, using my share of the investment, drilled an offset well near our big discovery well. He seemed to have "struck it" fairly well. I asked him what was my share, but he replied that because the new site idea was his, *none* of the proceeds would be mine, even though my money had been used in the special undertaking. I did not get upset, because when you're a slave of Jesus, it saves you a lot of worry and heartache. This was the Lord's problem, not mine; after all, everything I now owned had been given to Him. I explained to this partner that he was stealing the Lord's property, not mine. I prayed and moved on in the Lord's work. Later, I learned the former partner's very promising oil well had become swamped by salt water and ruined.

Slaves of Jesus hold loosely the treasures of life, not clinging to them as if they were a fortune, but spending them freely in following Him. As we go, we retain no guilt or anger if someone steals from us or abuses the property we have given over to the Master. Then there is no reason for us to be upset. We absorb the apparent "loss" and let the Lord balance out the matter in our life and in the life of the person who has wronged us. Living this way brings peace.

This perspective keeps our blood pressure down and our spirits up. "For everything comes from him; everything exists by his power and is intended for his glory. To him be glory evermore" (Rom. 11:36).

Our Master may give material goods to be managed and used by His slaves, but not to replace Him.

> *To his own master he stands or falls; and stand he will, for the Lord is able to make him stand (Rom. 14:4, NASB).*

Is there anything I have that I would not readily release if Jesus asked me to?

Peter explained that when we feel wronged, we are to let the Master handle our defense: "This suffering is all part of what God has called you to. Christ, who suffered for you, is your example. Follow in his steps. He never sinned, and he never deceived anyone. He did not retaliate when he was insulted. When he suffered, he did not threaten to get even. He left his case in the hands of God, who always judges fairly" (1 Pet. 2:21-23).

Slaves of Jesus who obey their Master choose not to be entangled in attacks against each other, of any kind! Paul warned that we are never to file a lawsuit against another child of God! "When you have something against another Christian, why do you file a lawsuit and ask a secular court to decide the matter, instead of taking it to other Christians to decide who is right?" (1 Cor. 6:1). Does that not include suing for divorce?

It has been a special joy for me to see the creation of "Christian arbitration" groups, led by Christians who are lawyers and who help other Christians settle their differences by agreement. Without rancor, they sit together and work out their differences.

Imagine if we all lived this way! Perhaps the world would say of us, as one historian did of first-century Christians, "See how they love each other!" Tertullian, an Early Church father, said, "It is our care for the helpless, our practice of lovingkindness, that brands us in the eyes of many of our opponents. . . . 'Look,' they say, 'How they love one another! Look how they are prepared to die for one another!'" Lucian (A.D. 120–200), a prominent unbelieving writer, observed loving Christians: "It is incredible to see the fervor with which the people of that religion help each other in their wants. They spare nothing. Their First Legislator [Jesus] has put into their heads that they are brethren."

The nearer we live to the examples of first-century Christians, the more likely we are to avoid battles with other Christians, and the more certain we are that Jesus alone is best qualified to handle attacks against us. Let it be said of us, "See how they love each other! See how they let their God defend them!"

Our Master expects His slaves to depend on Him for their defense.

> *And having been freed from sin, you became slaves of righteousness. . . . So now present your members as slaves to righteousness, resulting in sanctification. . . . For this is the will of God, your sanctification. . . . "Sanctify them in the truth; Your word is truth" (Rom. 6:18-19 NASB; 1 Thess. 4:3, NASB; John 17:17, NASB).*

Am I trusting the Lord to fight for me?

Why mince words? Any contact, relationship or arrangement that separates us from the Master, even for a moment, is not acceptable to our Lord. Sadly, many individuals spend their entire lives wandering here and there trying everything in vain pursuit of self-satisfaction. As a result, they end up in all sorts of business and personal relationships that are harmful, ungodly and without fruit, and lead basically to a dead-end existence.

Our Master expects His slaves to remain true to Him.

But now that you have come to know God, or rather to be known by God, how is it that you turn back again to the weak and worthless elemental things, to which you desire to be enslaved all over again? . . . For we also once were foolish ourselves, disobedient, deceived, enslaved to various lusts and pleasures, spending our life in malice and envy, hateful, hating one another (Gal. 4:9, NASB; Titus 3:3, NASB).

Do my relationships reflect negatively on my Master?

Slaves of Jesus know where they are NOT going! They do not travel the streets of lust, as we are warned in Proverbs 6:24-33 and 7:6-23. They know to flee adultery and fornication, as did Joseph (see Gen. 39:7); and in today's world, that means not turning the television channels to pornography, or renting X-rated movies or accessing Internet pornography sites! They do not join those who mock God, those who traffick in sin or those who counsel ungodly ideas (see Ps. 1). But they do assemble themselves together for mutual encouragement (see Heb. 10:25). They do study and meditate upon the Word of God and are spurred into "noble" partnerships as the Bereans of long ago (see Acts 17:11). As a result, they do enter a new dimension of living, a different level, a totally different plane of existence, an exciting adventure, a journey of obedience and faith that is full of love and peace.

Slaves know the will of the Master, because it is written down to be read and understood. Rightly, it has been said, "The Bible will keep you from sin, and sin will keep you from the Bible." The Holy Spirit is within us to help us discern its meaning and enable us to obey its precepts. For example, my frequent prayer about my relationship with Vonette is that God would take my life rather than allow me to act in any way that would grieve the Holy Spirit or be unfaithful to our marriage vows.

As I look around at the places I am going and at those with whom I am traveling, do they look vaguely familiar as haunts of the past—before the Master bought me and before I chose to enjoy being His slave? Alert to old dangers, I make sure my love-light is shining toward Him and His.

When I choose to recognize my role as a slave of Jesus, I do not lose the capacity to sin, but I am uncomfortable the very moment I sin. To guard against disobeying the Master, I need only look for certain signs. The first one will be my love; is it first and foremost for the Master? Other signs develop as I ask: Have I turned toward the old ways of competing, conniving and condemning others so I can look good? Is my motive lust, pride, personal gain or a desire to trump another slave's action?

Slaves of Jesus are new creatures who enjoy His mercies and faithfulness afresh each morning. They stay near the family of faith. There is no joy in leaving the household of being a slave of Jesus and turning back to enslavement to the flesh, to the old nature, to the dog-eat-dog, grind-it-out, be-in-charge life, and suffer the consequences. That lifestyle is not for the true slave. We can escape those dreadful ways by staying true to our decision to be slaves of Jesus, and being true to the Master who loves us so.

Paul said, "Forgetting the past and looking forward to what lies ahead, I strain to reach the end of the race and receive the prize for which God, through Christ Jesus, is calling us up to heaven" (Phil. 3:13-14). Slaves of Jesus expect the best is yet to be. The past is merely prologue to what God can do when we expect Him to move as we obey His commands and act upon His

promises. Never a dull moment! Think of it: the excitement of today and tomorrow, alive in Christ, forever! What a way to live!

Our Master expects His slaves to maintain their first love for Him.

> *The truth is, anyone who believes in me will do the same works
> I have done, and even greater works, because I am going to be
> with the Father. You can ask for anything in my name, and I
> will do it, because the work of the Son brings glory to the Fa-
> ther. Yes, ask anything in my name, and I will do it! (John
> 14:12-14).*

***Does my life reflect the Master's plans for me to love Him with
all my heart, mind, soul and strength?***

Do we really believe our Master said "greater works"? And
what do you think Jesus meant when He said these words: "I assure you, even if you had faith as small as a mustard seed you
could say to this mountain, 'Move from here to there,' and it
would move. Nothing would be impossible" (Matt. 17:20)? These
are supernatural words, and they make it clear that He wants His
followers to think supernaturally—to have the mindset that He
has. Figuratively, mountains of faith are moved every day as God
moves in His mysterious ways to honor our faith in Him and His
promises. Literally, some great land masses are moved as huge
earth-moving machines scoop up the earth after the mountain-
top has been dynamited. That soil is moved somewhere else to
help stabilize land for construction or preservation.

One of the creators of great earth-moving equipment was R.
G. LeTourneau of Texas. I went to visit him because He was
renowned for at least two things: the huge equipment his company created and the large percentage of his income given to the

Lord's work. I discovered machines as large as five-story buildings, and the heart of a man that was larger still. He said he became a tither, and as He did, God so blessed his business that he increased his giving to 20 percent, then 30 percent, then 50 percent and, finally, his tithing reached a point where he gave 90 percent! This man thought supernaturally! Using such instruments as a charitable remainder trust, he actually gave away most of his tens of millions of dollars of wealth. His testimony helped my faith grow by leaps and bounds. "Now glory be to God! By his mighty power at work within us, he is able to accomplish infinitely more than we would ever dare to ask or hope" (Eph. 3:20).

Slaves of Jesus keep their minds on what He can do supernaturally.

Christ in you the hope of glory. . . . It is no longer I who live, but Christ lives in me (Col. 1:27, NASB; Gal. 2:20, NASB).

Am I trusting God for supernatural insights each day?

The great biblical scholar J. B. Phillips, in his introduction to his translation of the New Testament Epistles, *Letters to Young Churches*, said the following:

The great difference between present-day Christianity and that of which we read in these letters is that to us it is primarily a performance; to them it was a real experience. We are apt to reduce the Christian religion to a code, or at best a rule of heart and life. To these men it is quite plainly the invasion of their lives by a new quality of life altogether. They do not hesitate to describe this as Christ "living in" them . . . Perhaps if we believed what they believed, we might achieve what they achieved.[1]

The Scriptures clearly teach that the One who created the heavens and the earth lived among us, died on a cross for our sins, rose again and now lives by His Spirit in the life of every believer. For the Christian, the purpose of life is not what we do for Christ, but what He does in and through us to accomplish His will, His way. But He must have our full allegiance and cooperation.

So I often pray, *Lord Jesus, I want to be a suit of clothes for You. I just want You to walk around in my body, think with my mind, love with my heart, speak with my lips, seek and save the lost through me; I'm just available.* The suit of clothes does not make things happen. It is Jesus as Lord who gives forgiveness, purpose, power and peace through the yielded life. Another illustration is that of a glove. Slaves are merely gloves through whom the Sovereign Master of the Universe can thrust His hand to transform lives. The glove does not make things move; His hand does.

Our Master is ready to fill and empower us as we surrender to Him.

But when the Holy Spirit has come upon you, you will receive power and will tell people about me everywhere—in Jerusalem, throughout Judea, in Samaria, and to the ends of the earth (Acts 1:8).

Am I experiencing this kind of relationship with my Master?

Paul presents other word pictures of this truth: "But this precious treasure—this light and power that now shine within us—is held in perishable containers, that is, in our weak bodies. So everyone can see that our glorious power is from God and is not our own" (2 Cor. 4:7). He reminds us, "Or don't you know that your body is the temple of the Holy Spirit, who lives in you and was given to you by God? You do not belong to yourself" (1 Cor. 6:19).

True Abundant Living

His Choice

Attitudes can deteriorate rapidly. But we have some simple instructions for how we can maintain the mindset of a slave by choice. In the next verses, list at least one way a believer can keep the right attitude about life.

Revelation 2:4-5

_____
_____
_____
_____

Philippians 3:13-14

_____
_____
_____
_____

Philippians 4:8

_____
_____
_____
_____

My Choice

The Bible gives practical suggestions on how to maintain these right attitudes for Jesus. Using each set of verses, name one way you can show the right attitude in each of these areas.

Think supernaturally (Eph. 3:20).

_____
_____
_____
_____

Let God handle the problem (Rom. 5:3-4).

_____

_____

_____

_____

Manage material possessions God's way (1 Cor. 4:2).

_____

_____

_____

_____

Don't retaliate against wrongs done to you (1 Cor. 6:1).

_____

_____

_____

_____

Keep yourself pure (Phil. 4:8).

_____

_____

_____

_____

Be empowered by God (2 Cor. 4:7).

_____

_____

_____

_____

Note

1. J.B. Phillips, *Letters to Young Churches* (De Soto, TX: Macmillan, 1947).

7

REFLECTING GOD'S LOVE

Choice Point
Show no sense of superiority over others.

My decision to become a "slave by choice" primarily was motivated by realizing how much God loves me. But where did that information come from? A major part of my understanding came from Paul's writings, especially to the believers in Christ at Ephesus, many of whom were slaves in physical fact. The city of Ephesus was one of the largest slave depots in the world. Its marketplace was at the very heart of global trafficking in human slavery. While walking around Ephesus, a person was likely to hear such questions as: "Whose slave are you?" "How much did he pay for you?" "When were you bought?" "How does he treat you?" "Are you going to leave him when your debt is paid?" And the masters would confer: "Where did you get that one?" "Is he a good worker?" "What's her attitude?" "How much did you pay?"

This backdrop brings to life the apostle Paul's letter to the Ephesians in which he celebrates the many benefits of belonging to Jesus. For me, the full awareness of these many acts of love by God in Christ awakened in me a strong desire to serve Jesus the way a slave serves his master, in complete and total submission to the master's will and in confident assurance of the Master's provision for me. Of course, we realize that all these benefits are part of what God gives to *every* Christian, whether or not they decide to recognize and act upon the liberating joy of spiritual slavery in Christ.

For me, it is not enough merely to read and acknowledge that my position before God is that of a slave, as Paul explained and exemplified. I choose to live in the reality of God's Word about spiritual slavery. How much more exhilarating it is to begin to *live* as a slave of Jesus, by faith, and to begin experiencing all of the benefits of belonging to Jesus. For example, you may have a fantastic automobile parked in your garage. You may sit in it, bask in its beauty and admire its features. You even may start the engine, hear the sounds of excellence in engineering and feel the power of its engine vibrations. But until you take it to the streets, you do not experience all that it means to be in that car! Dear friend, we are in Christ, who is the fullness of the Godhead bodily (see Col. 2:9)! We have every reason to enjoy our enslavement to Him as we let the Master reign in us everywhere we go!

To me, being a slave of Jesus is the most logical thing I can imagine. Here we are, indwelt by the great Creator-God and Savior who made all that is, all that we comprehend and infinitely more. Does it not seem downright foolish to deny such a matchless Master, with His unfathomable love, power, wisdom and knowledge, to direct our lives?

How Much We Cost

There is yet another way to look at the matter. For many people, one of the hardest facts of life to face is this: I do not own me; the Lord Jesus Christ owns me. But in considering yourself a slave for Jesus, it is a totally logical and intellectually satisfying realization. He bought and paid for me. I was in the slave market of sin—filthy and without a destination full of hope or a destiny full of joy. He gave His life for my ransom, and now I am His. Beware of those who offer you any Christless or Crossless philosophy.

> There will also be false teachers among you, who will secretly introduce destructive heresies, even denying the Master who bought them . . . for God bought you with a high price. So you must honor God with your body. . . . For you know that God paid a ransom to save you from the empty life you inherited from your ancestors. And the ran-

som he paid was not mere gold or silver. He paid for you with the precious lifeblood of Christ, the sinless, spotless Lamb of God (2 Pet. 2:1, *NASB*; 1 Cor. 6:20; 1 Pet. 1:18-19).

From time to time, my selfish nature, the "old me," may want to argue about this spiritual slavery. When it does, He presents the record—the full price paid in blood at Golgotha, a terrible crucifixion in Jerusalem 2,000 years ago. The record has an official seal upon it, authenticated by His empty tomb; He is not there, He is risen! The title deed of my life is marked: "Property of Jesus Christ." I can argue about who owns me to my lifelong frustration, or I can choose to accept His gracious and legal right to my life and enjoy being a member of His household, as a slave and as a friend.

Because we freely and gratefully accept being the property of God, we recognize that He has full authority over our lives. His ownership makes Him responsible for what happens to us. Like a tenant who can rely on the landlord to repair the house; we can depend upon our Master to take care of the body in which we dwell and to protect us wherever we go. He provides everything we need. "My God will supply all your needs according to His riches in glory in Christ Jesus" (Phil. 4:19, *NASB*). He is a wonderful Owner!

Marked for All to See

Shall we accept the branding that comes with belonging to Jesus? We have been elevated into His household and made a part of His royal family by the fact of His purchase of us out of the slave market of sin. The permanent upside is eternal and glorious—sharing the destiny or fate of our Lord. The temporary "downside" is occasional grief and persecution here on earth because we are identified as children of God.

The servant shares the master's fate. And since I, the master of the household, have been called the prince of demons, how much more will it happen to you, the members of the household! But don't be afraid of those who threaten you. For the time is coming when everything will be revealed; all that is secret will be made public (Matt. 10:25-26).

If we try to behave as if we are *not* His, we end up exactly like Peter did before the crucifixion of Jesus. Ordinary people in Jerusalem said, "Isn't he one of those who is with the Galilean?" They knew he belonged to Jesus, even when Peter denied it. A disobedient Christian fools no one—neither believers nor unbelievers. We are marked as the purchased possession, yes, the personal property, of almighty God!

Jesus has bought us out of slavery to sin, and we can expect one day to be sin-free in glory, which will be joy for us and praise to God the Father. We are His property. We have become God's own possession. We belong to Him, and the world knows it. The Holy Spirit Himself keeps guard on us as precious possessions of God. We can say, on the authority of the Master's Word, to the accuser of our souls, "Don't touch me; I belong to God; you cannot mess with me unless you get approval from my owner, my Master, the Lord Jesus Christ!" (see Jas. 4:7; Job 1:6-12).

This enables us to sleep well at night, for He watches over us. It keeps us from running in fear when we can walk in faith. It thrills our souls to know we belong to the great Savior and sovereign God of the universe, never to be lost, never to be without identity in Him!

A sense of belonging is one of the deep roots every person needs in order to thrive. To most, it is as important as knowing that your body and soul are safe. Because we belong to the Master, we rest confidently that He has ownership control, not just of our daily lives but also of our eternal destiny.

What a Family!

When God does anything, He does it right—all is thoroughly and completely finished, no dangling details undone. For example, when He accepts us into His family, He makes us all of one rank, first-class and fully endowed. He has adopted us, made us equal partakers in His will, and given us full access to His household.

The world may see me as fanatical, but the Master sees me as friend and member of His family. *This is the life!* He has even included me in His will! He has taken me into the Royal Family and made me feel like a king! I wonder what took me so long to surrender myself to Him!

A tiny glimmer of this wonderful relationship occurred in 1996, when Vonette and I approached Buckingham Palace not as tourists and visitors but as expected guests! For a moment, we were nervous. But as we approached the gates, we found ourselves not only admitted and welcomed but also fully accepted in the palace! It would have been enough to stop right there and enjoy the view! But we were escorted to a place of prominence; we had an appointment with Prince Phillip! "His majesty" brought us into his presence, and again we were accepted at a new level as never before. The next thing I knew, his royal highness was placing a gold medallion and a royal ribbon around my neck representing the Templeton Prize for Progress in Religion and with it a check for more than $1,050,000! Accepted! It was a little bit like when Vonette said yes, she would marry me! But all this is nothing compared to hearing our Lord Jesus say, "Well done, thou good and faithful slave."

Because we belong to Him, we have insider knowledge from the Master of the Universe. "Friendship with the LORD is reserved for those who fear him. With them he shares the secrets of his covenant" (Ps. 25:14). We have freedom to come and go into the courts of His Majesty. We are members of the Royal Family of God! The Master has given us full rights to all that is His! In the court of eternity, the will of our Master has been reviewed and the Judge has ruled we are fully entitled heirs. This is the most lucrative arrangement ever designed, and it is ours because of the benevolence and good will of the Master! All this and heaven too!

Privileges and Responsibilities

Because we belong to Jesus, we are entitled to share in all the privileges and responsibilities of being part of His family! Paul spent much of his letter to the Galatians explaining the difference between the old slavery and the new, between the laws of God, such as the Ten Commandments, which teach us our need of a Savior, and the grace of God that we find in Jesus as Master.

To the Ephesians, Paul begins, as he often did, with a greeting of "grace" followed by "peace." That is the sequence he always uses, because we can never know the peace of God until we have experienced the grace of God. Then he starts describing what it means to belong to Jesus. Paul was so in love with his Master that at the mention of the Lord's name, Paul was ready to write a book. An example occurs in his letter to Christians residing in the slave world of Ephesus. Paul wrote to them, and after his second reference to "our Lord Jesus Christ," his pen flew across the page. He began to cite a summary of the benefits of belonging to Jesus. In the original, verses 3-14 are one long sentence—the longest in the New Testament. The listing is certainly not all of the benefits, but what a start!

Paul's message was that God bought us out of the slave market of sin; He paid the ransom (slave price); He paid what we owed and could not pay; and we became His. *Now we belong to Him! Free to be His!* Now we are unbound slaves gratefully choosing to accept His control of our lives, and this transaction is joyful. We are relieved of the awful consequences and anxieties of our debt to sin. What a load off our minds and our backs! We were going to have to pay throughout eternity for the wrongness of our acts, for missing the mark, for failing to live up to the standards of a holy God, for letting ourselves down, for hurting others, for sinning! But Jesus "paid it all; all to Him I owe; Sin had left a crimson stain, He washed it white as snow!"[1]

Paul emphasizes the certainty of the fullness of our salvation by closing with further good news. The Holy Spirit Himself is the guarantee that God has purchased us, that we belong to Him, that Jesus has bought us out of slavery to sin, and we can expect one day to be sin-free in glory, which will be joy for us and praise to God the Father. We are His property. We have become "God's own possession" (1 Pet. 2:9, *NASB*). We belong to Him, and the world knows it. The Holy Spirit Himself keeps guard on us as precious possessions of God.

These concepts are rooted in the literal language Paul used. This passage forms a complete picture of what it means to escape sin's power and penalty and to choose the joy of being bound forever to the Master, Jesus Christ. All are found in most Bibles as "redeemed" or "bought."

The roots of being a slave of Jesus run deep, according to historical and biblical records. As early Christians began the revolution of living as slaves of Jesus, they were part of a culture of slaves. Here was a common way a person identified himself or herself: "I belong to (name of master)." In today's American English, some music fans across America may declare their loyalty to a particular rock group or star. They may say, "I belong to the Grateful Dead, or to Elvis Presley." It means people think constantly about the message of the one they listen to and worship. They will go anywhere to worship the object of their hearts. They will go into debt in order to be able to follow. They want to be so identified with their idols that it affects the clothes and jewelry they wear, the cars they drive and even the way they talk.

The discussion that the apostle Paul had with the Corinthians used this same slave language when he described them as saying, "One of you says, 'I am a follower of Paul,' and another says, 'I prefer Apollos'" (1 Cor. 3:4). This term also was used of belonging to political parties in the Roman era. Finally, it was common for runaway slaves to be branded across the forehead "I belong to (name of master); please return me." Their owners put a collar on them stating the name of the owner.

Christ's slave is continually seeking his Master's favor and will. As exemplified in the life of Paul, this can lead to dangerous situations as well as blessings. Riot and revival marked Paul's "enslavement" to Christ. Jailed and jeered, he was undeterred, because he insisted upon being "obedient to the heavenly vision" Jesus gave him. The prize of spiritual slavery is faithful reward, but the price of spiritual slavery often meant death. In the New Testament, there are 26 terms for crucifixion, and each one is used in connection with slavery.

A Summary of Benefits for Slaves of Jesus

In Ephesians 1:3-14, I find a clear summary of what it means to belong to Jesus. I am His chosen one, who gives praise to and receives joyful deeds from God. I am set apart from the world, sacred and not sinful. I was planned for (in Christ) and prioritized before time began. I am flawless in appearance and faultless in character. I was adopted into His family and given the highest status available. I am not only admitted but also accepted in the royal household in the front ranks and seated at the head table. I am blood ransomed out of the slavery of sin. I have an undeserved pardon from crime and unearned freedom from sin's bondage. I am unworthy as a worm yet wealthy as the King of kings. I have been certified with the imprint of authority by the Holy Spirit, once and for all, as personal property owned by Jesus the Messiah, who paid for me and preserves me.

Owned by Jesus

So, I have two questions: Can you think of any condition better than being a voluntary slave of Jesus? Can you imagine anything more exciting than being in the personal service of the King of the universe?

I cannot conceive of how the children of kings must feel, but I do know what it feels like to be a slave of King Jesus; it is wonderful beyond words to describe! I seem to see a record where He has placed my soul in the inventory of eternity, and one day when that record is opened for every eye to see, there is going to be a line under "Date Purchased," and the date will be approximately A.D. 33 when our Lord died in our place at Calvary. In the next column, under "Name" will be "Bill Bright," and then "place of birth—Coweta, Oklahoma." And another column will be entitled "Date Entered," and it will read: "April 1945, Hollywood, California," when I received

Him as my personal Lord and Savior. Another column will say, "Vocation," and it will say, "Slave by Choice." What joy it will be to see our names written there, in the Lamb's book of life (see Rev. 21:27)!

Called by His Love

The value of belonging to Him is illustrated by this true story involving William Booth, founder of the Salvation Army. At Christmas in nineteenth-century London, there was a tradition that each church would send messengers into the streets to invite the poor to Christmas celebrations, for food and fellowship in the household of faith. But the messengers soon began to discriminate by calling out: "All of you who are Anglicans, come with us."

Catholics announced, "All who are Catholics, come with us." The Methodists, the Lutherans, and other denominations and independent churches did the same.

The problem was that when all the invitations had been called, many more people remained without an invitation. That's when William Booth shouted to the city, "All of you who belong to no one, come with me."

Booth's invitation exactly echoed the command of his Master. Everyone who is willing can belong to Jesus. Everyone who has not been called by or who has not accepted the call of any other master is welcomed by our Lord Jesus, whose message this very day is: "Come, everyone, I want you to belong to Me."

The prophet Isaiah foresaw this relationship: "Some will proudly claim, 'I belong to the LORD'" (Isa. 44:5). Paul said we all have been "called to belong to Jesus Christ" (Rom. 1:6). As Lawrence O. Richards notes, "As those who belong to Jesus, we enter a new world of light."[2]

Choose Your Master Today

I invite you to ask God to take over control of your life. You can do this through prayer, which is talking with God. Even now, you can pray something like this (the words are not as important as the attitude of your heart):

Heavenly Father, today I choose to become Your slave. Master, I sur-
render control of my life to You. You show me the way to go and
what to do, and I will obey. I thank You for buying me out of the
slavery of sin and giving me the opportunity to serve as Your slave.
Lead me, Lord and Master; I will follow. In Jesus' name, make it so.

I want anyone who is not confident that God rewards obedience and provides for His slaves to be assured that He does. And if
telling you how faithful Christ has been in my life will encourage
you to live as a slave of Jesus, then accept God's inspired promise
as well as my testimony as evidence of who He is and how He will
provide for you. I can assure you, there is absolutely nothing to
fear when you surrender your life to Christ to become His slave.

Master-Slave Summary

Let me summarize briefly what the Word of God says, about the
master-slave relationship as a picture of the Christian life. An
outline of the master-slave relationship serves as a worthy outline
of the spiritual life:

1. Every human being is born into this world as a slave—
   a slave to sin. We are subject to a cruel and hateful
   tyrant, Satan himself, the enemy of God. We are indentured for time and eternity because we have no way
   to redeem ourselves out of our slavery to sin. (See John
   3:36; John 8:34,44; Rom. 1:18-20; 2:5; 6:23; 7:25; 1 Cor.
   6:9-11; Eph. 2:3; 1 John 5:19.)

2. Jesus Christ, the incomparable, peerless Son of God,
   was sent to earth by the Father to redeem those enslaved to Satan and to sin; to buy them for Himself by
   paying the price, with His own blood, for the sin that
   indentured them to Satan in the beginning. (See Luke
   4:18-19; John 3:16-17; Rom. 3:24; 1 Cor. 6:20; Gal. 3:13;
   Eph. 1:7; Col. 1:14; 1 Pet. 1:18-19; 2:1; 1 John 3:8.)

Bill and Vonette's wedding day, December 30, 1948, in Coweta, Oklahoma.

Miss Mears greeting a reception for Campus Crusade board members and staff (1954).

Henrietta Mears's home at 110 Stone Canyon Road, Bel Air, California.

Bill and Vonette Bright host a reception for Jerome Hines before a special performance at Arrowhead Springs, California (1965).

Bill talks with UCLA All-American athletes and Campus Crusade student leaders Bob Davenport, Rafer Johnson and Don Shennick (1955).

A family photo of Brad, Vonette, Bill and Zac after Brad's first haircut (1960).

The Bright family prepares for a family vacation (1968).

Billy Graham and Bill Bright at the Berkeley Blitz in Berkeley, California (1967).

Dedication of the Christian Embassy in Washington, D.C. (1974).

The Bright Family: Zac, Vonette, Bill and Brad (1958).

Dr. Bright speaking to UCLA students in Miss Mears's home (1960).

A fundraising banquet for Campus Crusade for Christ (1955).

Miss Mears with Bill, Brad and Zac (spring of 1962).

Dr. Bright with decathlon winner Rafer Johnson.

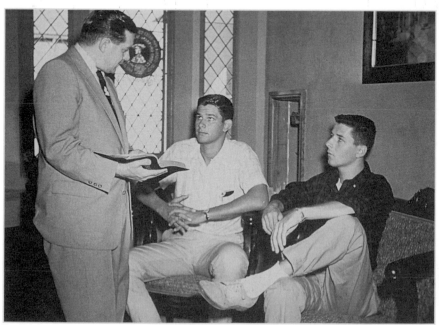

Dr. Bright discussing the Four Spiritual Laws with skeptical students.

Zac, Brad and Bill at First Presbyterian Church of San Bernardino, California.

Bill enjoys time with his sons, Zac and Brad, at the Forest Home Christian Conference grounds (1974).

Bill enjoying time at home in Arrowhead Springs, California (1982).

The Bright men: Brad, Bill and Zac (Christmas 1973).

Bright family photo (1972).

Bill helps Vonette in the kitchen at a family reunion in Coweta, Oklahoma (1979).

Final day of Explo '72. It is estimated that 250,000 attended the closing ceremony in Dallas, Texas.

Campus Crusade's nationwide *I found it!* campaign launched in 1972.

Dr. Bright greets Pope Paul VI in Rome (1996).

The *JESUS* film is shown in Bangalore, India, on a double-sided screen.

Brad, Vonette and Bill at Explo '74 in Korea. An estimated one and half million people attended.

The *I found it!* campaign materials included the Four Spiritual Laws.

I found it! billboards dotted the countryside across America (1976).

Vonette and Bill in front of St. Basil's Cathedral in Red Square, Moscow, Russia (1991).

Vonette and Bill take a garden walk—and talk, of course (1998).

The *JESUS* film, here showing in Madagascar, has reached countless individuals.

Vonette and Bill in front of Campus Crusade World Headquarters in Orlando, Florida.

Bill speaks at a Promise Keepers event in Indianapolis, Indiana, in 1994.

Bill Bright launching the *Here's Life, World* campaign.

Bill and Vonette have a family game night with their grandchildren.

Bill reading his Bible in a favorite chair at Arrowhead Springs, California (1993).

Bill and Vonette celebrate 50 years of marriage at a reception in Orlando, Florida.

Bill announces the transfer of leadership to Steve Douglass at Staff Training in Ft. Collins, Colorado (2001).

The prayerful dedication of Dr. Steve Douglass as president of Campus Crusade for Christ, International (2001).

Vonette embraces her favorite photo of Bill (2004).

3. First to be redeemed were a group of disciples who later became the apostles of Jesus. They were set free from enslavement to their cruel taskmaster (Satan), having been bought by the blood of Jesus. Though they now belonged to Jesus, they were not forced to serve Him. All but one voluntarily chose to live in the legal relationship resulting from Jesus' purchase of them. They volunteered to live as slaves by choice. (See Rom. 1:1; Gal. 1:10; Phil. 1:1; Col. 1:7; 4:12; 2 Pet. 1:1; Jude 1:1.)

4. Jesus, our Master, left this earth and returned to heaven. But before doing so, He gave the command and the authority to His apostles to go into all the world and, in His name, proclaim forgiveness to all who were enslaved by sin and who would receive the free gift of redemption through faith in Him. To all who accepted redemption, it was announced that they were now the property of a Master who has gone away but will return. There will be rewards for those slaves who are found living lives of obedient service to the Master when He returns, and rebuke for those not living obediently as His slaves. (See Matt. 25:14-30; 28:18-20; Luke 12:35-48; Acts 1:8.)

5. Succeeding generations of disciples, on the authority of the Master's original commission, have continued to proclaim the message of redemption paid for by the Master, Jesus. All believers of Jesus alive today have been purchased by His blood and are His property. But not all have chosen to live as obedient and faithful slaves. This failure accounts for the weakness we see in the Body of Christ—those who are redeemed by the blood of Christ, the church. (See Rom. 12:1-2; 1 Cor. 6:19-20; 7:21-23; Heb. 12:1-2.)

6. Knowing that the Master could return at any moment, individual slaves of Jesus are faced with a decision

that will affect their lives for the rest of their years on earth as well as for all eternity: Will they choose to serve the Master who bought them, or will they live as lazy, rebellious and disobedient slaves—enjoying the benefits of His household but carrying out none of the responsibilities thereof?

7. The many joys of being slaves of Jesus make it the greatest lifestyle on earth. The pressure is off slaves. They need only love, trust and obey the greatest Person who ever lived, Jesus of Nazareth, as their Master. As they do obey Him, their love grows, and they discover they can trust Him with more and more to help fulfill the Great Commission until He returns. Far from drudgery, this is a life of spiritual ecstasy because of the greatness and goodness of the Master.

8. The benefits of being a slave of Christ are awesome. We can spend our lives telling of the joy of sins forgiven, of protective peace, of the precious presence and power of the Holy Spirit, and of the thoughtfulness of our great Creator God and Savior, who planned before the beginning of time to buy us out of the marketplace of sin and redeem us by sending His only begotten Son to die for us. Think of the joy and earth-changing delight of it: spending our lives obeying His commands to love others and train others in all that He taught.

Becoming a Slave of Jesus

Have you made a decision to present yourself to God as a living sacrifice and to live as a slave of Christ until He returns? I am very concerned about the absence of meaningful commitment in the twenty-first-century body of professing believers in Jesus Christ. That is why I have written this book—to focus the church on thinking of the radical and complete surrender of ourselves to Jesus, which must be accompanied by a simultaneous rejection of comfort, materialism, fame or fortune as the driving motives of our lives.

I am convinced that according to God's Word, many professing Christians will not inherit eternal life as explained in 1 John 2:2-6, where the apostle John, writing under the inspiration of the Holy Spirit, records, "[Jesus] is the sacrifice for our sins. He takes away not only our sins but the sins of all the world. And how can we be sure that we belong to him? By obeying his commandments. If someone says, 'I belong to God,' but doesn't obey God's commandments, that person is a liar and does not live in the truth. But those who obey God's word really do love him. That is the way to know whether or not we live in him. Those who say they live in God should live their lives as Christ did."

If you have "left your first love" and have found you love things, money, popularity, good works and even the Church more than you love Jesus, I urge you to ask God to cleanse you and forgive you and make full surrender of your life to Christ now before it is too late to do so. Your very destiny—your eternal destiny—may well be at stake. You may think you are a believer, but the fact is, if you are *living in a pattern as though Christ did not pay the penalty for your sins,* it is likely that He is not even in your life.

Every professing follower of Christ must consider seriously the words of our Lord to His disciples recorded in Mark 8:34-38: "Then he called his disciples and the crowds to come over and listen. 'If any of you wants to be my follower,' he told them, 'you must put aside your selfish ambition, shoulder your cross, and follow me. If you try to keep your life for yourself, you will lose it. But if you give up your life for my sake and for the sake of the Good News, you will find true life. And how do you benefit if you gain the whole world but lose your own soul in the process? Is anything worth more than your soul? If a person is ashamed of my message in these adulterous and sinful days, I, the Son of Man, will be ashamed of that person when I return in the glory of my Father with the holy angels.'"

A Thought from Vonette

Our contract was simply two pages—his page and mine. Bill suggested as we went into separate rooms of our little cottage home in the Holly-wood hills that we make a list of what we wanted out of life, materially and spiritually. I was a two-and-a-half-year-old believer; Bill was about a five-and-a-half-year-old believer. I took him literally. My list con-sisted mostly of material specifics:

- Two to four children
- Two cars, mine could be a Ford (the least expensive at the time)
- A home modest enough that a person from skid row would be comfortable, and lovely enough to entertain the president of the United States
- The Proverbs 31 woman was my spiritual model
- I wanted to be totally committed to Christ and committed to my husband and his dreams and aspirations
- I wanted to be a woman of God led by the Holy Spirit and be and do what God wanted me to be and do
- Bill was my spiritual leader as my husband

Bill's list was brief as well, but his list was far more explicit spiri-tually than mine. As he has perfected that list, I can agree wholeheart-edly with the content. There was not a materialistic bone in Bill's body.

To me, it would be extremely important that a husband and wife come to agreement before signing the following contract.

Instead, this very day, please decide to join me and millions of others in experiencing the joy and benefits of becoming slaves of Je-sus. It is the choice of eternity. Do not miss it.

You have read in this book how Vonette and I formalized our decision to live as Christ's slaves by writing contracts that expressed our heart's desires and decision. We did that because we knew it helps to put significant decisions in writing. Written documents, especially the Word of God, become living standards to which we return time and time again when clarity and conviction are needed.

To that end, I suggest below a simple model statement that you can adapt and adopt as your own contract with God to live as a slave of Jesus Christ. Let me urge you today to submit yourself to Christ as His slave and to live out the rest of your life in obedience to the One who loves you and purchased you for Himself by the shedding of His blood on the cross. Everything I have related to you in this book—the words of Jesus, other teachings in Scripture, my own personal experience—points to the same conclusion: We can really and fully experience the joy, the love and the blessings of a free and meaningful life only as we fully surrender ourselves to our Lord Jesus Christ as His obedient slaves.

Contract as a Voluntary Slave of the Lord Jesus Christ

1. Desiring to live my life in accordance with the supernatural plans and purposes of God as revealed in Scripture, I choose to voluntarily submit myself to the Lord Jesus to live as His slave for the rest of my life.

2. As His slave, I will seek to maintain an intimate relationship with my Master by daily reading, studying, memorizing and meditating on His holy, inspired Word, the Bible.

3. I will seek with the help of the Holy Spirit to make prayer—for others as well as myself—a vital priority in my life.

4. As a faithful, trustworthy steward, I surrender to Him ownership of all property and resources that I now have, and whatever I may acquire in the future, dedicating them to be used for His glory and according to His direction.

5. I dedicate my body, time, talents, treasures, gifts and abilities to be used in Christ's service.

6. I trust Jesus Christ, as my faithful Master, to meet every personal and ministry need that may arise in the future. I choose to cast all my cares upon Him, knowing that He loves me and cares for me as demonstrated by His dying on the cross for me and being resurrected to live in me.

7. I choose to share the fate of my Master, Jesus Christ. If I am called to share in the fellowship of His sufferings, I will, with His strength do so with joy, knowing that my eternal life is secure and that He has prepared a place for me where I will dwell with Him forever.

8. I choose to be found active in my Master's service from this day forward until He returns. My ultimate goal in life is to bring maximum glory to Him.

9. Since Jesus came to seek and save the lost, I shall, with the enabling of the Holy Spirit, invite Him (Jesus) to continue seeking and saving the lost through me toward the fulfillment of the Great Commission.

10. I choose to rely upon the Holy Spirit to help me live a holy life. I will depend upon Him for strength, wisdom, power and grace to carry out the terms of this contract, dedicating myself not to grieve Him or quench His Spirit by willful sin, but rather to love, trust and obey God until my last breath is taken here on planet Earth.

_____   _____
Signed   Date

If you desire to sign this contract with Christ, or write out your own contract using similar language that expresses your decision, you may want to pause and pray as you commit your contract to God, asking Him to accept it in the good faith in which it was signed:

Holy heavenly Father, thank You for Your Son, the Lord Jesus Christ, who purchased me out of the marketplace of slavery to sin, and forgave my sin with the price of His own precious blood. I offer to You today this contract, this agreement, by which I choose to live the rest of my life as a slave of Christ. Please grant the presence and power of Your Holy Spirit to enable me to faithfully keep the provisions of this contract as I have expressed them to You. And please begin today to direct my steps into the place of service where I may allow Jesus to be Master as I seek to represent Him effectively. I pray for wisdom and direction in using the resources You have entrusted to me for the glory of my Master, Jesus Christ. I pray these things in His all-powerful, wonderful name, amen.

A Joyful Reunion of Fellow Slaves of Jesus

Thank you, dear friend, for your decision to live as a slave of Christ. And if you have not made that decision today, may I encourage you to continue considering it before the Lord in prayer in the days ahead. As I stated earlier, my only regret in making this decision in 1951 was that I had not made it sooner. I am confident that as you become a slave of Jesus, you will be liberated to enjoy the full, abundant and exciting life that Jesus promised to all who love, trust and obey Him—a life Vonette and I have enjoyed by His grace since 1951.

A moving image in the New Testament epistles is that of fellow slaves linked together in a yoke of obedient service to their Master, Jesus Christ. My wish is that I could embrace you in person as my fellow slave of our gracious Master, Jesus Christ. If I do not have that opportunity here on earth, we will embrace inside heaven's gate as we spend eternity recounting the faithfulness of our Master on earth and His glory in heaven. All glory, honor, worship and praise be to His name, forever and forever and forever, amen!

If you have made the liberating decision to enjoy being a slave of Jesus, to delight in belonging to the greatest personality of all time, please contact Vonette Bright: Campus Crusade for Christ, 100 Lake Hart Dr., Orlando, Florida, 32832; or email: vonette.bright@ccci.org.

For additional materials that I have written to enhance your journey with Christ, ask for your free copies of "Would You Like to Know God Personally?" and "Have You Made the Wonderful Discovery of the Spirit-filled Life?"

You will never regret formally taking action to declare you are a Royal Slave of Jesus. This decision helps make it plain for all to know that we have unconditionally surrendered to Christ; we have irrevocably committed ourselves to Him, and we expect to live under His ownership and Lordship.

For a crucial consideration of two subjects of overriding importance about voluntary spiritual slavery, please continue reading the final two chapters of this book.

Reflecting God's Love

His Choice

What does Job 1:6-12 tell us about our security in God's care?

_____

_____

_____

_____

_____

_____

What does God promise in Psalm 25:14?

_____

_____

_____

_____

_____

Using Ephesians 1:3-14, write down all the benefits the one who belongs to Jesus receives.

_____

_____

_____

_____

_____

What benefit do you find in Revelation 21:27?

_____

_____

_____

_____

_____

What will every believer have according to 1 John 2:1-3?

_____

_____

_____

_____

_____

Summarize the call Jesus makes to His followers as found in Mark 8:34-38.

_____

_____

_____

_____

_____

My Choice

A bond-servant in Roman times agreed to voluntarily serve his master for the rest of his life. He did this because of the love and dedication he had for his master. Many times, this came about because the master was so good to his slave.

Jesus is so much greater than any earthly master. He has of-
fered us so much, including eternal life. I urge you to be a slave by
choice for Jesus. If you want to make that commitment, reread
the contract in this chapter. Prayerfully consider each point and
the commitment it contains. Change any wording you feel God is
leading you to alter. Then sign and date the contract.

Make a copy of your contract, and put it in a place where you
can see it every day.

Notes
   1. "Jesus Paid It All," Elvina M. Hall (1820–1889).
   2. Lawrence O. Richards, *New International Encyclopedia of Bible Words* (Grand Rapids, MI:
      Zondervan Publishing House, 1991), p. 123.

8

THE BATTLE RAGES

Choice Point
Know that trouble will come, but trust the Master to handle it.

For the slave of Jesus, total surrender is not the end of spiritual growth; it is the beginning of spiritual warfare. Until you have surrendered your life, the enemy of our souls, Satan, pays little attention to you. But once you begin as a slave to walk in obedience to Jesus, you are truly a threat to the aims of the evil one. Slaves of Jesus must come to realize that every day is a time of spiritual conflict.

The Bible says, "The mind set on the flesh is hostile [at war] toward God; for it does not subject itself to the law of God, for it is not even able to do so, and those who are in the flesh cannot please God" (Rom. 8:7-8, *NASB*). The term "flesh" refers to our old nature without Christ. Until we received Him in the person of His Holy Spirit, we were unable even to recognize this battle-ground of the mind, and we were powerless to conquer powerful temptations such as pride, sex and materialism.

The first act of warfare is vigilance. Be on the lookout. "Be of sober spirit, be on the alert. Your adversary, the devil, prowls about like a roaring lion, seeking someone to devour" (1 Pet. 5:8, *NASB*). In the book of Judges, we see that God recruited a sharp but small band of warriors by testing them on their vigilance. He recruited and retained only those who drank from a stream by cupping their hands and *keeping their head and eyes up* at all times (see Judg. 7:6).

We need only take a brief look around and see one huge area of spiritual warfare where Satan is temporarily winning battles. For example, consider the lust of the flesh or the eye gate of the mind. Appealing to that area of our lives has become a $10 billion per year pornography industry in the United States. It sells more of its wares than the *combined* enterprises of the National Basketball Association (NBA) and the National Football League (NFL). Think of it! With $10 billion, the entire world can be reached for Christ in a single year. Instead, Satan has diverted those resources to the kingdom of darkness, seeking to reduce sacred sex to animal behaviors and to destroy and demean the godly role of women, whose stature always has been elevated wherever the cause of Christ has gone. "There is no longer Jew or Gentile, slave or free, male or female. For you are all Christians—you are one in Christ Jesus" (Gal. 3:28). "And further, you will submit to one another out of reverence for Christ" (Eph. 5:21).

That merely illustrates the scale and scope of spiritual warfare. Second, we must remember that the Bible says every person on planet Earth is either a citizen of Christ's kingdom or of Satan's kingdom. To which do you belong? There is no neutral ground. If you try to walk between two warring forces, you are likely to draw fire from both sides. The slave of Jesus celebrates that he or she is delivered from Satan's kingdom.

"For he has rescued us out of the darkness and gloom of Satan's kingdom and brought us into the kingdom of his dear Son, who bought our freedom with his blood and forgave us all our sins" (Col. 1:13-14, *TLB*). But there is an ongoing spiritual warfare with unseen forces. The Bible says, "For our struggle is not against flesh and blood, but against the rulers, against the powers, against the world forces of this darkness, against the spiritual forces of wickedness in the heavenly places" (Eph. 6:12, *NASB*).

So there are three types of people in this war zone: (1) those who overcome these evil forces by faith in Christ; (2) those who ignore the enemy and suffer casualties; or (3) those who object blindly to the very idea of the devil and spiritual warfare.

Satan's kingdom is characterized by these attributes: sexually immoral, impure, debauched, idolatrous, lustful, hostile, quarrelsome, jealous, angry, given to selfish ambition, conceited, envious, demonic, drunken, wild, deceitful, adulterous, given to homosexuality, greedy, given to lying and cheating (see Gal. 5:19-21). The chief characteristic of Satan's kingdom is rebellion and disobedience to godly authority. "And you were dead in your trespasses and sins, in which you formerly walked according to the course of this world, according to *the prince of the power of the air*, of the spirit that is now working in the *sons of disobedience*" (Eph 2:1-2, *NASB*, emphasis added).

"Rebel" and "disobey" have been the whispered and shouted watchwords of the enemy of our souls through the ages. Satan's various tactics include doubt, deceit, division, destruction, distraction, discouragement, depression, gossip, pornography, the undermining of godly authority, evil thoughts, instant gratification, coveting, and more.

Knowing the Enemy

His beginning was filled with such promise. He was described as "The Morning Star." His name meant "a bearer of light," and he was said to be the most beautiful and magnificent of all the angels created by God.

In fact, our Lord held him in high enough esteem to place him above all of the created order! This exalted being named Lucifer was assigned the task of passing on God's commands to all of the angels, then returning their worship to the Lord. Later, our sovereign and holy Lord sent this message to the one who began as "The Morning Star":

You were the perfection of wisdom and beauty. You were in Eden, the garden of God. . . . I ordained and anointed you as the mighty angelic guardian. You had access to the holy mountain of God and walked among the stones of fire. You were blameless in all you did from the day you were created until the day evil was found in you (Ezek. 28:12-15).

Evil found Lucifer, and Lucifer found evil. Evil is always a choice, and this dark angel, whom we now know as Satan, made the conscious decision to rebel against God. Sin is the result when any created being, including you or me, decides that he or she can become the ultimate master of his or her own life. Lucifer, filled with his false sense of greatness, attempted to claim a place in heaven higher than the throne of our Lord. Pride comes before a fall, and that may be the epitaph for the devil when our Lord finally locks him away and imprisons him for all eternity.

At the time of the rebellion, God expelled him from paradise and sent him to the lowest depths of creation:

How you are fallen from heaven, O shining star, son of the morning! You have been thrown down to the earth, you who destroyed the nations of the world. For you said to yourself, "I will ascend to heaven and set my throne above God's stars. I will preside on the mountain of the gods far away in the north. I will climb to the highest heavens and be like the Most High." But instead, you will be brought down to the place of the dead, down to its lowest depths (Isa. 14:12-15).

Since the day when Satan was cast out of heaven, evil has darkened this universe. The "Bearer of Light" became the Bringer of Darkness. So, when God created human beings for fellowship with Him, the devil wasted no time in coming to tempt them away from their loving Lord and Master. The third chapter of Genesis tells the story of how the devil succeeded in bringing about the sinful corruption of Adam and Eve in the Garden of Eden.

The devil, with the help of his fellow fallen angels (see Jude 1:6), continues to tempt God's children to this very day. His dark footprints can be followed all through the Scriptures to his unsuccessful tempting of Jesus in the wilderness and up to his final actions in the book of Revelation. Satan is never idle, even in the lives of slaves of Jesus.

The Certain Conflict

We must face the compelling truth that supernatural conflict is inevitable. Many Christians believe that the more they love, honor and serve our Lord, the less hardship and conflict life will hold. And there is a certain amount of truth to that idea. It is certainly true that when we busy ourselves serving God, we generally avoid the many entanglements of the world and its sinfulness. Our relationships improve. We are abundant in the fruit of the Spirit. We find joy and fulfillment in every aspect of life.

On the other hand, we must realize that temptations and trials will be a certainty. After all, the devil knows he need not waste his attention on nonbelievers or worldly, uncommitted Christians. They are presenting Satan with few problems, so why should he tempt them? In fact, they are contributing to his cause.

Spirit-filled Christians, on the other hand, provide a great headache for the devil! They thwart all his plans of disrupting the loving relationship between God and His children. Committed followers of Christ share their faith regularly and bring new believers to salvation, and there is nothing that upsets the devil more than that. Any one of these excited, Spirit-filled believers may turn out to be God's instrument for a new revival all across the world. The devil shudders to think there may be a new D. L. Moody or a successor to Billy Graham out there—maybe a number of them—maybe even you!

Satan will use all his tricks to cut off that possibility. He focuses all his attention on the Christians who are the most eager to serve God—those such as you who have decided to serve as slaves of Jesus.

Slaves Are Fearless

But please note from the very outset that, even as you acknowledge the active work of the devil, you should carry no fear of him.

"For God has not given us a spirit of fear and timidity, but of power, love, and self-discipline" (2 Tim. 1:7). Your loving and sovereign Lord, whose power is infinitely superior to that of the evil one, will always protect you. "But you belong to God, my dear children . . . the Spirit who lives in you is greater than the spirit who lives in the world" (1 John 4:4).

I know a young, gifted Christian who realized that God wanted to use him in a powerful way. But he was holding back his surrender to the Lordship of Christ for fear of how the devil would respond. It had come into his mind that if he moved forward in the service of Christ, Satan might take the life of this young man's father! Who but the devil himself would put such a thought into a believer's mind?

At the beginning of the book of Job, we see that the devil can do nothing apart from the boundaries set by God. "All right, you may test him," the LORD said to Satan. "Do whatever you want with everything he possesses, but don't harm him physically" (Job 1:12). Meanwhile, Jesus says, "I have given you authority over all the power of the enemy. . . . Nothing will injure you. But don't rejoice just because evil spirits obey you; rejoice because your names are registered as citizens of heaven" (Luke 10:19-20).

Why fear the devil? Our strength through our Lord is so much more powerful, and Satan has already been defeated at the cross. Remember the words of our Lord: "I give them eternal life, and they will never perish. No one will snatch them away from me, for my Father has given them to me, and he is more powerful than anyone else. So no one can take them from me" (John 10:28-29).

No, we need never fear the devil—but we must know his wily ways.

Satan's Strategies

In Genesis 3, we see that the devil's first maneuver was to *raise doubt* about the certainty of God's word. He asked Eve, "Did God really say you must not eat any of the fruit in the garden?" (Gen. 3:1). God had commanded no such thing; He had simply forbidden Adam and Eve to eat the fruit of the one tree (see Gen. 2:16-17).

When this approach failed, the next strategy was to *twist words in a lie* about God's Word: "You won't die!" the serpent hissed (Gen. 3:4), contradicting God's clear promise. And from there, once the authority of God's Word was eroded, Eve and Adam were open to the devil's attack by *appealing to their pride*. He wants us to give in to pride, just as he did, and usurp God's rightful place as ruler of our lives. So he offers the big lie: "You will become just like God, knowing everything, both good and evil" (Gen. 3:5).

The Garden of Eden story shows us the devil's pattern. He tests to see if we *know* God's Word; then he tests to see if we *trust* it; then he tests to see if we will *obey* it.

In the narrative of Jesus in the wilderness (see Matt. 4:11), we learn even more about the devil's approach. First he tempted Jesus through *physical appetites,* telling Him to turn the stones into bread (see vv. 3-4); next he tempted Him in the *realm of pride* or fame, suggesting that Jesus leap off the temple to be borne safely by angels (see vv. 5-6); and finally, he temped Christ to *take a shortcut away from His mission* and bow down to the devil in *immediate* exchange for the nations of the world and all their glory (see vv. 7-10). This appeal to *instant gratification* is a hallmark of Satan's devices. But Jesus knew He had to go to the cross, and He would not be detoured.

The devil knew that these were all twisted versions of the supernatural thoughts of Jesus. His bread, after all, was not conjured from stone, but was the bread of life. He did not intend to leap from the temple, but to become its replacement, our ultimate priest; and He did indeed have an eye toward the nations of the world, not through selling out to Satan, but through equipping His followers with the power of the Holy Spirit: "But when the Holy Spirit has come upon you, you will receive power and will tell people about me everywhere—in Jerusalem, throughout Judea, in Samaria, and to the ends of the earth" (Acts 1:8).

In summary, the devil will attack your obedience to God and His Word. By becoming a slave of Jesus, you will be tested in a way similar to the way Jesus was tempted in the wilderness. The devil will attempt to twist and subvert your thoughts. He will try to turn your thoughts, emotions and energies to his own ends. But while Adam and Eve gave in to the devil's shrewd suggestions, we can succeed like Jesus. For He Himself, living within us, will give us the power to overcome any temptation. As you allow the Holy Spirit to guide your thinking, you will experience His strength and His wisdom against the worst attacks of the devil. Simply walking by faith as a slave of Jesus means you will have a higher level of spiritual discernment; you will recognize the devil's schemes for what they are.

Secure in the Savior

By contrast, Christ's kingdom is as if from another world. It is characterized by "love, joy, peace, patience, kindness, goodness, faithfulness, gentleness and self-control" (Gal. 5:22-23). Jesus said, "The thief comes only to steal and kill and destroy; I came that they may have life, and have it abundantly" (John 10:10, *NASB*). Christ's ways are of self-denial (see Mark 8:34), love, delayed gratification, sacrifice for others, encouragement, support for godly authority, thoughts of purity, honesty, justice and goodness, among many others.

God has delivered followers of Christ from the forces of darkness into His kingdom of light. "For he has rescued us from the one who rules in the kingdom of darkness, and he has brought us into the Kingdom of his dear Son. God has purchased our freedom with his blood and has forgiven all our sins" (Col. 1:13-14).

Jesus said, "I am sending you, to open their eyes so that they may turn from darkness to light and from the dominion of Satan to God, that they may receive forgiveness of sins and an inheritance among those who have been sanctified by faith in Me" (Acts 26:17-18, *NASB*). And Paul, being the slave of Jesus that he was, testified, "I did not prove disobedient to the heavenly vision" (Acts 26:19, *NASB*).

The Believer's Victory

Through His death and resurrection, Jesus Christ conquered the forces of darkness and sealed their fate: "The Son of God appeared for this purpose, to destroy the works of the devil" (1 John 3:8, *NASB*).

It is our Lord alone who has the power to conquer satanic plans: "Therefore, since the children share in flesh and blood, He Himself likewise also partook of the same, that through death He might render powerless him who had the power of death, that is, the devil" (Heb. 2:14, *NASB*).

Jesus said, "Then the King will turn to those on the left and say, 'Away with you, you cursed ones, into the eternal fire prepared for the Devil and his demons!'" (Matt. 25:41).

God has destined a place for the devil and his minions: hell. That is the reason for the existence of hell: "And the devil who deceived them was thrown into the lake of fire and brimstone, where the beast and the false prophet are also; and they will be tormented day and night forever and ever" (Rev. 20:10, *NASB*).

The Battle Rages

But until that final day, forces of darkness, though doomed, still seek to destroy the lives of Christians. Jesus described some of Satan's goals this way: "The thief comes only to steal and kill and destroy" (John 10:10, *NASB*). The devil may attack your reputation, for example, to steal your good name, or your finances to rob you of joy. Such "theft" and "destruction" are from the evil one, as he may have appealed to our fleshly nature through lust and covetousness to trap us into his destructive schemes.

> Put on the full armor of God, so that you will be able to stand firm against the schemes of the devil (Eph. 6:11, *NASB*).

> He was a murderer from the beginning, and does not stand in the truth because there is no truth in him.

Whenever he speaks a lie, he speaks from his own nature,
for he is a liar and the father of lies (John 8:44, *NASB*).

Our enemies are the world, the flesh, and satanic forces seeking
to thwart God's wonderful plan for our lives.

We know that we are children of God and that the world
around us is under the power and control of the evil one
(1 John 5:19).

For all that is in the world, the lust of the flesh and the
lust of the eyes and the boastful pride of life, is not
from the Father, but is from the world (1 John 2:16,
NASB).

Beloved, I urge you as aliens and strangers to abstain
from fleshly lusts which wage war against the soul (1 Pet.
2:11, *NASB*).

For the mind set on the flesh is death, but the mind set
on the Spirit is life and peace, because the mind set on the
flesh is hostile toward God; for it does not subject itself
to the law of God, for it is not even able to do so (Rom.
8:6-7, *NASB*).

This is the judgment, that the Light has come into the
world, and men loved the darkness rather than the Light,
for their deeds were evil (John 3:19, *NASB*).

Don't let us yield to temptation, but deliver us from the
evil one (Matt. 6:13).

So now we can tell who are children of God and who are
children of the Devil. Anyone who does not obey God's
commands and does not love other Christians does not
belong to God (1 John 3:10).

The Believer's Armor

Followers of Christ are victoriously equipped for daily warfare through faith. Here are some of the promises of God to claim in the spiritual warfare:

But the Lord is faithful; he will make you strong and guard you from the evil one (2 Thess. 3:3).

Greater is he that is in you, than he that is in the world (1 John 4:4, *KJV*).

For since He Himself was tempted in that which He has suffered, He is able to come to the aid of those who are tempted (Heb. 2:18, *NASB*).

Take up the full armor of God, so that you will be able to resist in the evil day, and having done everything, to stand firm. Stand firm therefore, having girded your loins with the belt of truth, and having put on the breastplate of righteousness, and having shod your feet with the preparation of the gospel of peace; in addition to all, taking up the shield of faith with which you will be able to extinguish all the flaming arrows of the evil one. And take the helmet of salvation and the sword of the Spirit, which is the word of God (Eph. 6:13-17, *NASB*).

No temptation has overtaken you but such as is common to man; and God is faithful, who will not allow you to be tempted beyond what you are able, but with the temptation will provide the way of escape also, so that you will be able to endure it (1 Cor. 10:13, *NASB*).

Marching Orders

Christians are *not* to "hold the fort" or "hold out"; they are to advance God's kingdom in spite of evil spiritual forces. Consider our orders from the Lord of all:

Do not be overcome by evil, but overcome evil with good (Rom. 12:21, *NASB*).

I will build my church, and the powers of hell will not conquer it (Matt. 16:18).

Let your light shine before men in such a way that they may see your good works, and glorify your Father who is in heaven (Matt. 5:16, *NASB*).

All authority has been given to Me in heaven and on earth. Go therefore and make disciples of all the nations, baptizing them in the name of the Father and the Son and the Holy Spirit, teaching them to observe all that I commanded you; and I am with you always, even to the end of the age (Matt. 28:18-20, *NASB*).

Submit therefore to God. Resist the devil and he will flee from you (Jas. 4:7, *NASB*).

Behold, I have given you authority . . . over all the power of the enemy, and nothing will injure you (Luke 10:19, *NASB*).

With all prayer and petition pray at all times in the Spirit, and with this in view, be on the alert with all perseverance and petition for all the saints (Eph. 6:18, *NASB*).

A final guide in all things is this: If unclear as to the correct course of action, pray and then exert the love of God by faith in all situations. Here is history's best description of that love: "Love is patient and kind. Love is not jealous or boastful or proud or rude. Love does not demand its own way. Love is not irritable, and it keeps no record of when it has been wronged. It is never glad about injustice but rejoices whenever the truth wins out. Love never gives up, never loses faith, is always hopeful, and endures through every circumstance. Love will last forever" (1 Cor. 13:4-8). In so doing, you can be sure of victory, because God's love never fails.

Slaves of Jesus are always training and growing. And here is their daily agenda: G-R-O-W-T-H.

G   Go to God in prayer. Talk to Him each day (see Phil. 4:6-7).

R   Read God's Word every day. It will build your faith (see 2 Tim. 3:16-17).

O   Obey God as an expression of your love for Him (see John 14:21).

W   Witness—tell others about Christ by your life and words (see Col. 1:25-28).

T   Trust God with every detail of your life (see 1 Pet. 5:7).

H   Holy Spirit—this is God's Spirit living in you. Invite Him to give you His power to live your life and tell others (Gal. 5:16-18; Acts 1:8).

May God continually empower you as you claim victories in the spiritual warfare of your daily life.

The Battle Rages

His Choice

What is the relationship between the unbeliever and God (see Rom. 8:7-8)?

_____

_____

_____

_____

_____

What is the Christian's first act of warfare against Satan (see 1 Pet. 5:8)?

_____

_____

_____

_____

_____

Who wins the battle (see Heb. 2:14)?

_____

_____

_____

_____

_____

_____

What three types of temptations do we humans face (see 1 John 2:16)?

_____

_____

_____

_____

_____

_____

My Choice

How am I supposed to face spiritual warfare (see 2 Tim. 1:7)?

_____

_____

_____

_____

_____

What are the pieces of armor God has given you to be victorious (see Eph. 6:13-17)?

1. _____

2. _____

3. _____

4. _____

5. _____

6. _____

How can prayer help us in spiritual warfare (see Eph. 6:18)?

_____

_____

_____

_____

_____

_____

What promise do you have about temptations (see 1 Cor. 10:13)?

_____

_____

_____

_____

_____

_____

Copy the G-R-O-W-T-H chart given in this chapter and use it daily to help you resist temptation and to heal the brokenhearted.

9

SUPERNATURAL THINKING

Choice Point
Influence society as you rely on the Master.

Slaves of Jesus become supernatural soldiers of spiritual thought who are committed to help fulfill the Great Commission in their lifetime. They have a totally different mindset. They think supernaturally by always asking what almighty God can do. They stop to ask: What is our sovereign God doing in this particular battle?

Delivered from darkness and walking in the light of Christ, they have a mission. The apostle Paul, in his earliest letter to first-century Christians (circa A.D. 52), wrote, "But let us who live in the light think clearly, protected by the body armor of faith and love, and wearing as our helmet the confidence of our salvation" (1 Thess. 5:8).

Prepare for Spiritual Warfare

How then, can you prepare for spiritual warfare as a supernatural thinker? The following are several ways.

Memorize the Key Biblical Passages on Temptation

As you hide God's Word in your heart, the Holy Spirit will remind you again and again of God's power and promises during crucial moments of testing. Here are key passages for your reflection and memorization: James 1:2-5,12-16; 1 Peter 1:7; Matthew 14:38; 1 Corinthians 10:13; 1 John 4:4. Also, be sure to memorize the verses concerning the armor of faith: Ephesians 6:10-18.

Reflect daily upon the armor of faith, visualizing each part of the spiritual "equipment" and how it will protect you in the midst of that day's trials.

Pray Constantly

The closing verse of the armor of faith passage reads, "Pray at all times and on every occasion in the power of the Holy Spirit. Stay alert and be persistent in your prayers for all Christians everywhere" (Eph. 6:18). When Jesus faced temptation in the wilderness, and then in Gethsemane, He concentrated on prayer to keep His heart and mind focused on the purposes of God. The supernatural thinker prays naturally, instinctively, at all times. He or she constantly practices the presence of God and faces trials and temptations at full strength. "Always be joyful. Keep on praying. No matter what happens, always be thankful, for this is God's will for you who belong to Christ Jesus" (1 Thess. 5:16-18). Memorize and claim daily this promise from Philippians:

> Don't worry about anything; instead, pray about everything. Tell God what you need, and thank him for all he has done. If you do this, you will experience God's peace, which is far more wonderful than the human mind can understand. His peace will guard your hearts and minds as you live in Christ Jesus (Phil. 4:6-7).

Practice Spiritual Breathing

The moment you do anything to grieve or quench the Holy Spirit, *exhale*: confess it—no matter how large or small the act of disobedience. Accept the total forgiveness of Christ. "But if we confess our sins to him, he is faithful and just to forgive us and to cleanse us from every wrong" (1 John 1:9). Then *inhale*: appropriate the fullness and power of the Holy Spirit by faith. Always be certain that you are living in the wonderful experience of the Spirit-filled life. Ask Him to orchestrate your every attitude, motive, thought, desire, action or word. "If we are living now by the Holy Spirit, let us follow the Holy Spirit's leading in every part of our lives" (Gal. 5:25).

Overcome Evil with Good

"Don't let evil get the best of you, but conquer evil by doing good" (Rom. 12:21). Stay busy serving God. Keep witnessing, sharing the gospel with everyone you know, and focus on the fulfillment of the Great Commission in this generation. Immerse yourself in God's purpose for your life, and always walk in the Spirit. And when evil lies in your path, either as temptation or obstruction, stand firm in the power of our almighty, sovereign God who reigns over all creation. Satan has never won any victory over the Lord, and he has already lost the battle of Calvary. His defeat has been accomplished. Therefore, there will never be an occasion when you cannot overcome evil with good. Move forward in confidence and joy, and set your sights on supernatural victory.

The greatest joy in all the world is to be counted worthy by our Lord of playing a part in fulfilling supernatural achievements for Him. I am so humbled, and so thankful to God, that He has used someone as unworthy and insignificant as me in His great scheme of things, to play a role in His fantastic plans for this world. There is no other life I would ever want to lead. But what about you? Are you ready to believe God for impossible goals? I have given a very brief description of what my life has been like in that regard—what would yours be like?

Mission: Possible

Stop and try to imagine it—the kind of life we have been describing throughout this book. Can you even begin to visualize what your life would look like and feel like if you began to live as a slave of Jesus, thinking supernaturally for God?

The world is desperately in need of such achievers. God is searching for such a person. As we have seen, His eyes move to and fro throughout the earth, looking for the one who is willing to step forward and say, "Here am I, Lord. Send me." If you have read this far, I trust and pray that you are that person. I trust and pray that even now, you can see yourself stepping forward from a throng as wide as all humanity, saying:

Lord and Master, I trust You completely. I love You exclusively.
I am Your slave and I want to obey Your every command. Even
if no one else follows, and no one else chooses to live the super-
natural life, I will serve You as long as You will use me. Here am
I—send me and empower me to achieve impossible, supernatu-
ral goals for Your eternal glory and Your immediate kingdom.

Indeed, if you decide to think with a supernatural mindset and live the supernatural life, to trust God for the impossible, you will be a member of a very exclusive group. Few are those who are willing to give themselves absolutely and wholeheartedly to the amazing adventure of complete abandonment, as His slaves, to God's will and leadership.

I pray that the Holy Spirit has used the words of this book to challenge you and cause you to see your life in a completely different perspective. "Anything is possible if a person believes" (Mark 9:23). "Humanly speaking, it is impossible. But not with God. Everything is possible with God" (Mark 10:27).

The longer I live, the more I see that I have spent more than enough time doing just that: "humanly speaking." It is time for us to begin thinking and speaking the language of heaven. That language contains no word for "impossible." God longs to see you and me live as He intended us to live, breaking down new barriers and casting aside new obstacles each day as we achieve greater and greater wonders for Him. The writer of Hebrews is referring to just such a life in this passage:

Therefore, since we are surrounded by such a huge crowd of witnesses to the life of faith, let us strip off every weight that slows us down, especially the sin that so easily hinders our progress. And let us run with endurance the race that God has set before us. We do this by keeping our eyes on Jesus, on whom our faith depends from start to finish (Heb. 12:1-2).

When you begin to run that race, you will indeed begin to strip off and throw away all the hindrances that slow you down.

You will find yourself giving up some of the lesser pursuits that once seemed important. You may find that you have less time for television and the daily newspaper or some other lesser pastime that no longer holds any flavor or attraction for you. The Spirit of God allows testing of your character and refining of your desires. He will draw you onward toward the true essence of your life—the reason why He put you on this earth. You will have had a taste of the supernatural life, of trusting God for the impossible. From now until God calls you home, no other lifestyle will hold any appeal for you.

Let us close this book by taking a closer look at what your life will become after you have committed yourself to our great God who can achieve His amazing purposes through you.

Seeing Life God's Way

As you begin to live with the supernatural mindset that God always intended you to have, your whole world will begin to change. The great change will begin with the way you see your surroundings. You will look at the world as God sees it. You will be thinking with the mind of Christ. The Holy Spirit will hold such firm control of your life that you will be amazed to consider the thoughts you used to have and the perceptions that used to occur to you.

All around you, as you see through the eyes of heaven, you will visualize tasks that God wants done. You will see needs that must be filled, goals that must be reached and people who long to be loved and chaperoned joyfully into the presence of God. Not a single one of these tasks will seem to be a burden or a heavy responsibility, for the Spirit of God will fill you with joy and compassion, wisdom and strength for the task.

Then, as you begin to take on the challenges that God shows you, He will lead others to gather around you. You will be amazed by the wonderful people whom God sends across your path, because the world is one great pasture of billions of sheep without a Shepherd. The Lord will send you mentors to teach you, students to learn from you and caregivers to minister to your own needs. You will be part of a dynamic and loving community of faith, through church and through the many relationships God gives you. You will constantly be encouraging others, and you will constantly be encouraged.

Quite frequently you will find yourself sharing your faith with nonbelievers. Like the apostle Paul, you will find yourself saying, "Everywhere we go we tell everyone about Christ" (Col. 1:28). And like Philip who shared his faith with the Ethiopian, as recorded in Acts 8, you will find that the Spirit of God will place you in strategic places at strategic times for people who are in crisis, who are being drawn to the love of God. You will smile each time you realize God has maneuvered you into another setting of great opportunity. As you dynamically share your faith and introduce others to Christ, you will feel the joy of the most satisfying reward life has to offer. Those whom you lead to Christ will lead others to new life, and you will have the thrill of seeing new generations of God's children come into His kingdom.

You will find yourself serving more and more at the point of your gifts, for the Holy Spirit always works through the special spiritual gifts He has given us. As you do more for God, those gifts and skills will be sharpened. They will dovetail perfectly with the needs that loom in your path as you walk in the Spirit. You will discover new gifts you never knew you had.

Then you will see them—goals ahead of you that the world counts as impossible. The Lord will place them on your mind and heart until they begin to burn within you. A great burden will develop until you know for certain that God wants you to take on these goals for Him. Perhaps He wants to send you to another part of the world. Perhaps He wants to send you to a brand-new work in life. Perhaps there is some new achievement that has never before been accomplished, and God has been saving it just for you.

You can be certain that there is such a grand vision for your life, and that God has been saving it for you since before you were born, just as God spoke to Jeremiah: "I knew you before I formed you in your mother's womb. Before you were born I set you apart and appointed you as my spokesman to the world" (Jer. 1:5). Again, He said to Jeremiah, as recorded in Jeremiah 33:3, "Ask me and I will tell you some remarkable secrets about what is going to happen here" (Jer. 33:3).

Jeremiah was no different from you or me. Just as God had a task for that prophet to accomplish, He has a great task for you— or perhaps a whole series of them!

Seize the Joy

I challenge you to embrace today the excitement of that great work God has reserved for you. Feel the thrill of knowing there is at least one great victory that lies ahead for you, that the Lord placed it there with your name on it, and that in His strength all things are possible; all victories are certain.

I challenge you to thank God today for the new life that lies ahead for you, a life of supernatural vision and high achievement. Praise His name for the people who are living in darkness, who are bound to see a great light because God will use you to lead them to it. Believe me, you cannot even begin to imagine the wonders that lie in store for you as you make yourself available for His use. I can imagine the great smile He has as He thinks of the purposes for which He has set you apart.

This last promise is the best of all. As you walk boldly and thankfully into that future for which He has designed your life, you will come to know the Lord as you have never imagined it possible to know Him. This is surely the most supernatural achievement of all—that tiny, flawed human beings such as you or I could be counted worthy of the fellowship of the King, the One who created this universe and holds all creation in His hand. According to the passage above, His plans include your seeking Him and finding Him.

Whatever your present goals may be, finding an intimate walk with our Lord is the greatest joy there is. Knowing His love is the richest treasure you could find. Living in His power is life's most marvelous, amazing adventure.

A Thought from Vonette

I remember Bill telling someone, "Once we understand our new identity and invite Christ to live His life in and through us, joy will abound. Joy is a fruit produced by Christ's Spirit working in us (see Gal. 5:22). An apple tree—if it is healthy and receives a sufficient amount of sunshine, water and nutrients—will bear apples. It was created and designed for that purpose. In the same way, if we, as children of God, depend on the Holy Spirit to feed and nourish us, we will experience the fruit of joy in our lives."

"For I know the plans I have for you," says the Lord. "They are plans for good and not for disaster, to give you a future and a hope. In those days when you pray, I will listen. If you look for me in earnest, you will find me when you seek me. I will be found by you," says the Lord (Jer. 29:11-14).

As I leave you with these thoughts, my fervent prayers and my greatest encouragement, let us take one more look at the master plan for believing God for the impossible for supernatural living. I pray that you will set it within your heart, undergirded by His Word and your commitment to live it out.

Agree with the amazing truth that all things are possible in Christ! Begin ridding your mind of the world's misperceptions about what is or is not possible. Every day of your life, remind yourself that there are no limits to what God can do and wants to do through us. There are no boundaries or limitations to what He can do through us if we are willing to obediently surrender to His sovereign will and His guidance.

The adventure begins this very moment, as you give your heart to Christ in total obedience. This is no momentary feeling or temporary emotion—this is the foundation of every instant, every hour, every day and year of the rest of your life. I pray that you will take this moment to make a covenant with God that you will think, pray, play, love and live supernaturally from this day forward as a slave of Jesus.

Supernatural Thinking

His Choice

What descriptions does Paul give for the person who desires to serve God with his whole heart (see Heb. 12:2)?

_____
_____
_____
_____
_____
_____

What will a slave by choice do every day (see Phil. 4:4)?

_____
_____
_____
_____
_____
_____

What does God give us to help us serve Him? (Compare John 1:17 with 1 Cor. 12:4-11.)

_____
_____
_____
_____
_____

What promise does God give those who serve Him (see Jer. 29:11-14)?

_____
_____
_____
_____
_____

My Choice

To become a supernatural thinker, take these four steps:

1. Memorize passages on resisting temptation.
   Jas. 1:2-5; 1 Cor. 10:13; 1 John 4:4

2. Pray constantly.
   Eph. 6:18; 1 Thess. 5:16-18

3. Practice spiritual breathing.
   Exhale—confess each sin (1 John 1:9)
   Inhale—ask to be filled with the Holy Spirit (Eph. 5:18)

4. Overcome evil with good by sharing the gospel with others, walking in the Spirit, and standing firm against evil (see Col. 1:28; Gal. 5:16,25; Heb. 12:2).

APPENDIX A

HOW TO KNOW GOD PERSONALLY

Adapted from *Would You Like to Know God Personally?* a version of the Four Spiritual Laws written by Bill Bright. © 2007 Bright Media Foundation and Campus Crusade for Christ, Inc., Orlando, Florida.

Just as there are physical laws that govern the physical universe, so are there spiritual laws that govern your relationship with God.

LAW 1: *God loves you and offers a wonderful plan for your life.*

God's Love

"God so loved the world that He gave His one and only Son, that whoever believes in Him shall not perish but have eternal life" (John 3:16, NIV).

God's Plan

[Christ speaking] "I came that they might have life, and might have it abundantly" [that it might be full and meaningful] (John 10:10).

Why is it that most people are not experiencing the abundant life? Because...

LAW 2: *Man is sinful and separated from God. Therefore, he cannot know and experience God's love and plan for his life.*

Man Is Sinful

"All have sinned and fall short of the glory of God" (Romans 3:23).

Man was created to have fellowship with God; but, because of his own stubborn self-will, he chose to go his own independent way and fellowship with God was broken. This self-will, characterized by an attitude of active rebellion or passive indifference, is an evidence of what the Bible calls sin.

Man Is Separated
"The wages of sin is death" [spiritual separation from God] (Romans 6:23).

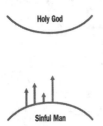

This diagram illustrates that God is holy and man is sinful. A great gulf separates the two. The arrows illustrate that man is continually trying to reach God and the abundant life through his own efforts, such as a good life, philosophy, or religion—but he inevitably fails.

The third law explains the only way to bridge this gulf...

LAW 3: *Jesus Christ is God's **only** provision for man's sin. Through Him you can know and experience God's love and plan for your life.*

He Died In Our Place
"God demonstrates His own love toward us, in that while we were yet sinners, Christ died for us" (Romans 5:8).

He Is the Only Way to God
"Jesus said to him, 'I am the way, and the truth, and the life; no one comes to the Father but through Me'" (John 14:6).

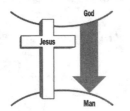

This diagram illustrates that God has bridged the gulf that separates us from Him by sending His Son, Jesus Christ, to die on the cross in our place to pay the penalty for our sins.

It is not enough just to know these three laws...

LAW 4: *We must individually **receive** Jesus Christ as Savior and Lord; then we can know and experience God's love and plan for our lives.*

We Must Receive Christ
"As many as received Him, to them He gave the right to become children of God, even to those who believe in His name" (John 1:12).

We Receive Christ Through Faith
"By grace you have been saved through faith; and that not of yourselves, it is the gift of God; not as a result of works, that no one should boast" (Ephesians 2:8,9).

When We Receive Christ, We Experience a New Birth
(Read John 3:1–8.)

We Receive Christ Through Personal Invitation

[Christ speaking] "Behold, I stand at the door and knock; if anyone hears My voice and opens the door, I will come in to him" (Revelation 3:20).

Receiving Christ involves turning to God from self (repentance) and trusting Christ to come into our lives to forgive our sins and to make us what He wants us to be. Just to agree intellectually that Jesus Christ is the Son of God and that He died on the cross for our sins is not enough. Nor is it enough to have an emotional experience. We receive Jesus Christ by faith, as an act of the will.

These two circles represent two kinds of lives:

Self-Directed Life
S – Self is on the throne
† – Christ is outside the life
● – Interests are directed by self, often resulting in discord and frustration

Christ-Directed Life
† – Christ is in the life and on the throne
S – Self is yielding to Christ
● – Interests are directed by Christ, resulting in harmony with God's plan

Which circle best represents your life?

Which circle would you like to have represent your life?

The following explains how you can receive Christ:

You Can Receive Christ Right Now by Faith Through Prayer
(Prayer is talking with God)

God knows your heart and is not so concerned with your words as He is with the attitude of your heart. The following is a suggested prayer:

> *Lord Jesus, I need You. Thank You for dying on the cross for my sins. I open the door of my life and receive You as my Savior and Lord. Thank You for forgiving my sins and giving me eternal life. Take control of the throne of my life. Make me the kind of person You want me to be.*

Does this prayer express the desire of your heart? If it does, I invite you to pray this prayer right now, and Christ will come into your life, as He promised.

How to Know That Christ Is in Your Life

Did you receive Christ into your life? According to His promise in Revelation 3:20, where is Christ right now in relation to you? Christ said that He would come into your life. Would He mislead you? On what authority do you know that God has answered your prayer? (The trustworthiness of God Himself and His Word.)

The Bible Promises Eternal Life to All Who Receive Christ

"God has given us eternal life, and this life is in His Son. He who has the Son has the life; he who does not have the Son of God does not have the life" (1 John 5:11,12).

Thank God often that Christ is in your life and that He will never leave you (Hebrews 13:5). You can know on the basis of His promise that Christ lives in you and that you have eternal life from the very moment you invite Him in. He will not deceive you.

An important reminder…

Do Not Depend on Feelings

The promise of God's Word, the Bible—not our feelings—is our authority. The Christian lives by faith (trust) in the trustworthiness of God Himself and His Word. This train diagram illustrates the relationship among fact (God and His Word), faith (our trust in God and His Word), and feeling (the result of our faith and obedience). (Read John 14:21.)

The train will run with or without the caboose. However, it would be useless to attempt to pull the train by the caboose. In the same way, as Christians we do not depend on feelings or emotions, but we place our faith (trust) in the trustworthiness of God and the promises of His Word.

Now That You Have Received Christ

The moment you received Christ by faith, as an act of the will, many things happened, including the following:

- Christ came into your life (Revelation 3:20; Colossians 1:27).
- Your sins were forgiven (Colossians 1:14).
- You became a child of God (John 1:12).
- You received eternal life (John 5:24).
- You began the great adventure for which God created you (John 10:10).

Can you think of anything more wonderful that could happen to you than receiving Christ? Would you like to thank God in prayer right now for what He has done for you? By thanking God, you demonstrate your faith.

To enjoy your new life to the fullest...

Suggestions for Christian Growth

Spiritual growth results from trusting Jesus Christ. A life of faith will enable you to trust God increasingly with every detail of your life, and to practice the following:

G *Go* to God in prayer daily (John 15:7).

R *Read* God's Word daily (Acts 17:11); begin with the Gospel of John.

O *Obey* God moment by moment (John 14:21).

W *Witness* for Christ by your life and words (Matthew 4:19; John 15:8).

T *Trust* God for every detail of your life (1 Peter 5:7).

H *Holy Spirit*—allow Him to control and empower your daily life and witness (Galatians 5:16,17; Acts 1:8; Ephesians 5:18).

Fellowship in a Good Church

God's Word instructs us not to forsake "the assembling of ourselves together" (Hebrews 10:25). If you do not belong to a church, do not wait to be invited. Take the initiative; call the pastor of a nearby church where Christ is honored and His Word is preached. Start this week, and make plans to attend regularly.

APPENDIX B

HOW TO BE FILLED WITH THE HOLY SPIRIT

Adapted from *Have You Made the Wonderful Discovery of the Spirit-filled Life?* Written by Bill Bright. ©1966, 1995, Campus Crusade for Christ, Inc., Orlando, Florida.

Every day can be an exciting adventure for the Christian who knows the reality of being filled with the Holy Spirit and who lives constantly, moment by moment, under His gracious direction.

The Bible tells us that there are three kinds of people:

1. **Natural Man:** One who has not received Christ.

"A natural man does not accept the things of the Spirit of God; for they are foolishness to him, and he cannot understand them, because they are spiritually appraised" (1 Corinthians 2:14, NASB).

Self-Directed Life
S – Self is on the throne
† – Christ is outside the life
● – Interests are directed by self, often resulting in discord and frustration **†**

2. **Spiritual Man:** One who is directed and empowered by the Holy Spirit.

"He who is spiritual appraises all things" (1 Corinthians 2:15, NASB).

Christ-Directed Life
S – Christ is in the life and on the throne
† – Self is yielding to Christ
● – Interests are directed by Christ, resulting in harmony with God's plan

3. **Carnal Man:** One who has received Christ, but who lives in defeat because he trusts in his own efforts to live the Christian life.

"I, brethren, could not speak to you as to spiritual people but as to carnal, as to babes in Christ. I fed you with milk and not with solid food; for until now you were not able to receive it, and even now you are still not able;

Self-Directed Life
S – Self is on the throne
† – Christ dethroned and not allowed to direct the life
● – Interests are directed by self, often resulting in discord and frustration

for you are still carnal. For when there are envy, strife, and divisions among you, are you not carnal and behaving like mere men?" (1 Corinthians 3:1–3).

The following are four principles for living the Spirit-filled life:

1 God has provided for us an abundant and fruitful Christian life.

"Jesus said, 'I have come that they may have life, and that they may have it more abundantly'" (John 10:10, NKJ).

"The fruit of the Spirit is love, joy, peace, patience, kindness, goodness, faithfulness, gentleness, self-control; against such things there is no law" (Galatians 5:22,23).

Read John 15:5 and Acts 1:8.

The following are some personal traits of the spiritual man that result from trusting God:

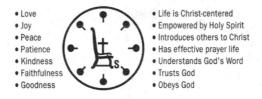

● Love
● Joy
● Peace
● Patience
● Kindness
● Faithfulness
● Goodness

● Life is Christ-centered
● Empowered by Holy Spirit
● Introduces others to Christ
● Has effective prayer life
● Understands God's Word
● Trusts God
● Obeys God

The degree to which these traits are manifested in the life depends on the extent to which the Christian trusts the Lord with every detail of his life, and on his maturity in Christ. One who is only beginning to understand the ministry of the Holy Spirit should not be discouraged if he is not as fruitful as more mature Christians who have known and experienced this truth for a longer period.

Why is it that most Christians are not experiencing the abundant life?

2 Carnal Christians cannot experience the abundant and fruitful Christian life.

The carnal man trusts in his own efforts to live the Christian life:

- He is either uninformed about, or has forgotten, God's love, forgiveness, and power (Romans 5:8–10; Hebrews 10:1–25; 1 John 1; 2:1–3; 2 Peter 1:9).
- He has an up-and-down spiritual experience.
- He wants to do what is right, but cannot.
- He fails to draw on the power of the Holy Spirit to live the Christian life (1 Corinthians 3:1–3; Romans 7:15–24; 8:7; Galatians 5:16–18).

Some or all of the following traits may characterize the carnal man—the Christian who does not fully trust God:

- Legalistic attitude
- Impure thoughts
- Jealousy
- Guilt
- Worry
- Discouragement
- Critical spirit
- Frustration

- Aimlessness
- Fear
- Ignorance of his spiritual heritage
- Unbelief
- Disobedience
- Loss of love for God and for others
- Poor prayer life
- No desire for Bible study

(The individual who professes to be a Christian but who continues to practice sin should realize that he may not be a Christian at all, according to 1 John 2:3; 3:6–9; and Ephesians 5:5.)

The third truth gives us the only solution to this problem...

3 Jesus promised the abundant and fruitful life as the result of being filled (directed and empowered) by the Holy Spirit.

The Spirit-filled life is the Christ-directed life by which Christ lives His life in and through us in the power of the Holy Spirit (John 15).

- One becomes a Christian through the ministry of the Holy Spirit (John 3:1–8.) From the moment of spiritual birth, the Christian is indwelt by the Holy Spirit at all times (John 1:12; Colossians 2:9,10; John 14:16,17).

  All Christians are indwelt by the Holy Spirit, but not all Christians are filled (directed, controlled, and empowered) by the Holy Spirit on an ongoing basis.

- The Holy Spirit is the source of the overflowing life (John 7:37–39).

- In His last command before His ascension, Christ promised the power of the Holy Spirit to enable us to be witnesses for Him (Acts 1:1–9).

How, then, can one be filled with the Holy Spirit?

4 We are filled (directed and empowered) by the Holy Spirit by faith; then we can experience the abundant and fruitful life that Christ promised to each Christian.

You can appropriate the filling of the Holy Spirit right now if you:

- Sincerely desire to be directed and empowered by the Holy Spirit (Matthew 5:6; John 7:37–39).
- Confess your sins. By faith, thank God that He has forgiven all of your sins—past, present, and future—because Christ died for you (Colossians 2:13–15).
- Present every area of your life to God (Romans 12:1,2).
- By faith claim the fullness of the Holy Spirit, according to:

  His command: Be filled with the Spirit. "Do not get drunk on wine, which leads to debauchery. Instead, be filled with the Spirit" (Ephesians 5:18).

  His promise: He will always answer when we pray according to His will. "This is the confidence we have in approaching God: that if we ask anything according to his will, he hears us. And if we know that He hears us—whatever we ask—we know that we have what we asked of Him" (1 John 5:14,15).

How to Pray in Faith to be Filled With the Holy Spirit

We are filled with the Holy Spirit by faith alone. However, true prayer is one way of expressing your faith. The following is a suggested prayer:

Dear Father, I need You. I acknowledge that I have been directing my own life and that, as a result, I have sinned against You. I thank You that You have forgiven my sins through Christ's death on the cross for me. I now invite Christ to again take His place on the throne of my life. Fill me with the Holy Spirit as You commanded me to be filled, and as You promised in Your Word that You would do if I asked in faith. I pray this in the name of Jesus. As an expression of my faith, I now thank You for directing my life and for filling me with the Holy Spirit.

Does this prayer express the desire of your heart? If so, bow in prayer and trust God to fill you with the Holy Spirit right now.

BILL BRIGHT: A SLAVE FOR CHRIST

By Michael Little, CBN President

He is best known for taking the gospel of Jesus Christ to the intelligentsia of the world—the students and professors of our universities. You may not recognize his face, but 139 million people around the globe know Jesus Christ as their Savior because of his ministry, Campus Crusade for Christ International.

For 50 years, Campus Crusade's founder, Bill Bright, has had one uncompromising passion: take the gospel of Jesus Christ to the world. That passion has resulted in 4.2 billion people hearing the life-changing message of Christ through the ministry of Campus Crusade. According to *Money Magazine,* Campus Crusade has been labeled the most "efficient" religious organization in the U.S.

It also ranks as the largest religious charity in America. Today, Campus Crusade has 25,000 full-time employees—the majority of which raise their own support. Another 553,700 people in 191 countries work as trained volunteers.

When you sit down with Bill Bright, as Christian Broadcasting Network President Michael Little did, you don't get a sense of his own incredible achievements but a profound sense of the greatness of his God. He is a humble man. A dedicated servant of his Lord and Master. Now, as he approaches the age of 80, he is battling pulmonary fibrosis, a medically incurable disease.

His adventure in ministry started back in 1951, while he was attending Fuller Theological Seminary. Out of a domestic dispute with his wife came a contract with God. In that contract both Brights pledged to become "slaves for Christ." It was a beginning that has impacted the world.

Michael Little: You and your wife have signed a contract with each other and with God saying, "We surrender ourselves to be slaves."

Bill Bright: Absolutely.

Little: Surrendering all, ownership, titles or to be . . .

Bright: Everything.

Little: . . . used in our useful lives as slaves of God.

Bright: I've never received a dollar royalty for any of my books because I feel, as a slave, everything that I have is a gift of my master.

Little: So is it like a vow of poverty?

Bright: I wouldn't say it's a vow of poverty in the sense that I ended up in some primitive part of the world, in a hut somewhere. But God and His sovereignty had a plan, and then took us immediately within a few months to the University of California Los Angeles campus. We rented a very nice home to entertain the students. And then we moved in with Dr. [Henrietta] Mears for nine years in a palace-type Moorish castle three minutes from the heart of the campus. And then we moved to Arrowhead Springs. So I couldn't say that I've lived the life of a deprived person.

Little: Doesn't sound like it.

Bright: The fact is, we assumed that was possible when we signed the contract and we've been prepared for that all through the years.

Little: But this contract surrendering to be a slave; is this something that you require of other followers?

Bright: I've never required it of anyone, though a good percentage of the people with whom I work have done it on their own initiative. Because frankly, when you study in the Scripture, the Scripture clearly teaches we're not our own. We've been bought with a price, the precious blood of the Lord Jesus Christ. So none of us really have any rights. I'm simply acknowledging that when I say, "Lord, I want to be Your slave." I know I'm a son of God, an heir of God, and a joint-heir of Christ. I'm seated with Him in the heavenlies, but by choice; like Paul, Peter and others, I've chosen to be a slave. And it's the most liberating thing you can imagine. All of these years now, I've seen this move grow for Vonette and myself.

Little: So the ministry Campus Crusade for Christ sort of spun out of this decision to surrender to be a slave?

Bright: Within 24 hours God had given me the vision.

Little: Was this your name? Would you name the ministry this? Campus Crusade?

Bright: I shared it the next day with a professor at Fuller Theological Seminary, Wilbur Smith, one of my favorite New Testament scholars. I shared with him what God had said to me the night before. And he got out of his chair in his office, paced back and forth; all he could say for about 30 minutes was, "This is of God. This is of God. This is of God." But then the next morning he came to class and he said, "God gave me the name for you—your vision." And he scribbled on a little piece of paper CCC, under which he wrote "Campus Crusade for Christ," and that's our name.

Little: Have you ever felt that name was limiting because you haven't been limited to campus to work?

Bright: We have 70 ministries. Some are marriage related; some have to do with the *JESUS* film in 600 languages. People have said to me, "Why don't you change your name?" And I've said, "Fine, come up with a better name and we'll change it." But no one has done that.

Little: No one has ever said the "Bill Bright Evangelistic Association"? You wouldn't have gone for that?

Bright: Us slaves don't have those things. So it's the emphasis on Jesus. So for 50 years we've talked about Him.

Little: You're looking back now 50 years, what has been the thing, which you look back and say, "That was just a standout event"? Maybe it's a rally in Seoul, Korea, or Dallas, Texas?

Bright: In Seoul, Korea, one night, I spoke to about 1.3 million people, and over a million of them indicated salvation decisions. They had a philosophy. Many of the Korean pastors told me that many were not sure of their salvation. They asked me to speak on Ephesians 2:8: "For by grace you have been saved through faith." Many wonderful people had been active church members but they weren't sure. They were trying to earn their salvation by their good works. On another occasion in Korea, in 1980, there were about 2 to 3 million every night in the meetings.

Little: Would you say that the *JESUS* film has won more people to Christ?

Bright: There have been over 4.2 billion in 645 languages in 235 countries believe the film. We have reason to believe there are hundreds of millions who have made some kind of decision.

Little: Sometimes I've read as many as one-third of the people who view it actually pray to receive.

Bright: I've seen occasions where most of the people present did that.

Little: Yes.

Bright: I remember a pastor of a large church in Nairobi, Kenya, wanted to start a new church. So we took the film to a part of the city where there was a lot of foot traffic and started the film. No one there but us. Soon there were about 1,500 people stopped to see it. And when the invitation was given, over half of them indicated they wanted to receive the Lord. So we started the church immediately.

Little: Just like that?

Bright: You know about the Dawn Ministry?

Little: Yes, sure.

Bright: Mr. Steele said their reports indicate that through the *JESUS* film and other evangelism in which we were involved, over 750,000 churches have been started. 750,000. So, this is what the Master does, not the slave.

Little: How would you describe yourself, theologically or doctrinally? Are you an ecumenical, are you an evangelical, how do you answer that question?

Bright: I'm a classical Christian.

Little: "Classical Christian."

Bright: I'm a New Testament Christian. I reject and throw out titles. I'm not a fundamentalist, though I'm fundamental in all of my doctrine. I'm not an evangelical, because that means that I exclude the Catholics and mainliners and Orthodox. I'm a believer who loves Jesus, and I work with everybody else whatever their denomination—Catholic, Orthodox, charismatic, mainline, evangelicals—anyone who loves Jesus, I'll work with them.

Little: Your family was involved in politics back in Oklahoma years ago. Campus Crusade is known for its influence throughout the evangelical, the larger Christian world. What is your stance politically? What involvement do you have politically?

Bright: I believe every Christian should be involved in politics—from the precinct to the White House. But we as a movement have chosen not to be partisan because we represent millions of people who share different views but they love Jesus. I'm more concerned about the salvation of souls than I am in promoting a particular party. But I'm a very conservative person politically. I abhor the murder of 40 million unborn babies. I deplore the pornography and all of the immoral, degenerate things that are happening in our country. I favor candidates who are biblically oriented, who hold the views of the Ten Commandments. I remember when Ronald Reagan was president he said, "If the American people obeyed the Ten Commandments and the Golden Rule we wouldn't have any problems." The first time I heard him say it I thought, *That's too simplistic.* There are complicated problems back there. But you analyze it, he's right. Every morning as I read the Scripture, every night, I quote the Ten Commandments and the Golden Rule.

Little: As a part of your devotional life?

Bright: I've just written a book on the Ten Commandments. Part of my devotional life, because I want before God that everything, every thought, attitude, action, motive, desire in my heart be pleasing to Him. I ask Him, "Keep the spotlight of Your Spirit on me so there would be nothing impure or unholy in my life." That's been my prayer for 50 years.

Little: By every measure, Campus Crusade for Christ has been a terrific success. Fifty-plus years, hundreds of millions of people have heard the gospel and have accepted Christ as a result of the multifaceted ministry. But there were hard lessons. Not everything has been positive.

Bright: Hardly.

Little: Well, what were the hard lessons of ministry life that you've had to learn?

Bright: Well, I had to learn how to trust the Lord. My faith muscles grew. Just like when you're exercising your muscles and they may be sore for a while, but they become stronger with exercise. Faith grows with exercise. You see God work miracles.

Little: Yes.

Bright: You're believing for more and so through the years God has honored that.

Little: But there's got to have been people sometimes in your life who have criticized you and said, "Our confidence is not in you, Bill Bright. We don't want you to be our leader." I remember one of those stories. Others who said you were a liberal, a heretic for associating with those outside of Protestantism. But what did that do to you?

Bright: Well, if you're referring to the document that I signed with Chuck Colson and others to embrace our fellow believers in the Roman Catholic tradition, they were the people who wrote me some very uncomplimentary letters. But I wrote back to tell them that I love them because the Scripture commands me to do that.

Little: Yes.

Bright: You know, you love God with all your heart, soul and mind, and you love your neighbor as yourself . . . and you love your enemies. So I've never allowed those critics to bother me. I just simply did what I believe God wanted me to do. Remember that I became a slave in 1951. Slaves have to obey their masters.

Note

1. Michael Little, "Bill Bright: A Slave for Christ," CBN.com, May 21, 2001. http://www.cbn. com/SpiritualLife/churchandministry/Bill_Bright_A_Slave_For_Christ.aspx.

NO INVOLUNTARY SERVITUDE

By Bill Bright

The very mention of the word "slave" to most American and European audiences calls to mind an image of the sinful slavery practiced in the United States and Europe for more than 100 years. That kind of involuntary slavery, indeed, was awful. That slave was considered mere property, like a horse, for example. It was terribly wrong, as the Bible states, and America fought a costly civil war to support former President Abraham Lincoln's "Emancipation Proclamation," which was the first official unlocking of the chains of slavery in the U.S. Lincoln, a dedicated Christian, was a faithful student of the Bible.

This is why followers of Christ began and won the battles for the abolition of slavery in Western civilization. Fearless preachers of the gospel of Jesus Christ, such as William Wilberforce, proclaimed the truth of the Bible opposing slavery and helped bring an end to this abominable practice (see Gal. 3:28; Eph. 2:14). That war is still being waged in many third-world countries.

Let me be as clear as I know how to be about this vital political issue: Although some scholars say the New Testament is "neutral" about slavery, I believe their analysis is incomplete and does not take into account the overriding commands of the Lord Jesus Christ to love others as God loves us, to do good to all men, to live out the Sermon on the Mount, to practice the Golden Rule. I find human slavery repugnant, morally indefensible, contrary to Jesus' teaching, and a practice never to support in any way. I believe Jesus died for slave owners and slaves alike and that He intended, as Paul summarized: "There is no longer Jew or Gentile, slave or free, male or female. For you are all Christians—you are one in Christ Jesus" (Gal. 3:28).

The Bible was written for all people of the world, for all time, in all social and economic conditions. At the time it was written, its readers included many who were slave owners and many more who were slaves of various types. The Greeks had their form of slavery, which was more moderate than brutal. The Israelites had a far more civilized form of slavery (usually not more than six years in duration, for example). The Romans had a distinctive multi-track caste system of slaves: The slave's treatment depended entirely on the political status of the Master, so that many slaves of the highly placed Romans had more privileges and even political power than free commoners.

The Bible does not duck the fact of human slavery, but rather its writers chose to use the fact as a metaphor to show the love of God. Our Lord Jesus Christ, the Son of God, comes disguised as a slave to fallen humanity. He sets us free by paying our sin debt—and He proclaims the love-status available to those who submit to Jesus as complete slaves.

In no way do I intend any aspect of this book to be construed as support of human slavery today nor to condone the practices of civilizations now gone from the earth. Further, I urge all thoughtful followers of Christ, committed to be "salt and light" in this life, to support anti-slavery movements in places throughout the world. May I urge you to prayerfully consider supporting abolition movements everywhere? An estimated 2.7 million persons are enslaved on planet Earth, according to the U.S. State Department, the United Nations and the Anti-Slavery Society. Of course, this does not include multiplied millions who reside in countries ruled by tyrants, nor the large numbers of persons currently involved in sex trafficking, especially in Asia.

Please pray for the physical and spiritual freedom of these oppressed persons.

BIBLIOGRAPHY

Greene, Michael P. *Illustrations of Biblical Preaching.* Grand Rapids, MI: Baker Book House, 1996.

Hawthorne, Gerald F. and Ralph P. Martin, eds. *Dictionary of Paul and His Letters.* Downer's Grove, IL: Intervarsity Press, 1993.

Hubbard, David Allan. *Beyond Futility.* Grand Rapids, MI: William B. Eerdmans Publishing Company, 1976.

Moulton, James Hope and William Francis Howard. *A Grammar of New Testament Greek: Accidence and Word Formation,* vol. II. Edinburgh, Scotland: T&T Clark, 1956.

Oversen-Norman Associates, The. *The New Testament and Wycliffe Bible Commentary.* New York, 1971.

Richards, Lawrence O. *New International Encyclopedia of Bible Words.* Grand Rapids, MI: Zondervan Publishing House, 1991.

Segalini, Erik. "Life Lessons" *Worldwide Challenge* magazine, Campus Crusade for Christ, January/February 2001.

Smith, William. *A Dictionary of the Bible.* Thomas Nelson Publishers, Nashville, TN, 1986.

Strong, James. *The New Strong's Exhaustive Concordance of the Bible.* Nashville, TN: Thomas Nelson, 1991.

Thomas, Dr. Alan Tomlinson, Professor of New Testament Theology, Midwestern Baptist Theological Seminary, Kansas City. Notes from years of studies on site in Italy, Greece and Turkey.

Vine, W.E., Merrill F. Unger and William White, Jr. *Vine's Complete Expository Dictionary of Old and New Testament Words.* Nashville, TN: Thomas Nelson, 1996.

Wuest, Kenneth. *Wuest's Word Studies from the Greek New Testament.* Grand Rapids, MI: William. B. Eerdmans Publishing Co., 1975.

WILLIAM R. BRIGHT

Founder, Chairman and President Emeritus
Campus Crusade for Christ International

Dr. Bright insisted on stating that all that he has been able to do was "entirely and completely because of the matchless grace of our incomparable Creator God and Savior; to Him be all the glory, honor, worship and praise." From a small beginning in 1951, the organization he began now has a presence in 196 countries in areas representing 99.6 percent of the world's population. Campus Crusade for Christ has more than 70 ministries and major projects, involving more than 25,000 full-time and 500,000 trained volunteer staff. Each ministry is designed to help fulfill the Great Commission: Christ's command to help carry the gospel of God's love and forgiveness in Christ to every person on earth.

Born in Coweta, Oklahoma, on October 19, 1921, Bright graduated with honors from Northeastern State University and did five years of graduate study at Princeton and Fuller Theological Seminaries. He was awarded eight honorary doctorate degrees from prestigious institutions and received numerous other recognitions, including the ECPA Gold Medallion Lifetime

Achievement Award (2001), the Golden Angel Award as International Churchman of the Year (1982), and the $1.1 million Templeton Prize for Progress in Religion (1996), which he dedicated to promoting fasting and prayer to help fulfill the Great Commission. He also won the Gold Medallion for his book *Witnessing Without Fear*. (His biography, *Amazing Faith*, by Michael Richardson, also won a Gold Medallion.) He received the first Lifetime Achievement Award granted by his alma mater (2001).

Bright is author of more than 100 books, booklets and scores of videos and audio tapes, as well as thousands of magazine articles and 2.6 billion copies of "The Four Spiritual Laws" in more than 200 major languages. His idea for the motion picture *JESUS* exploded into more than 812 languages seen by 5.6 billion persons in 236 nations, territories and provinces, as of July 2003.

Among his books are: *Come Help Change the World*; *The Secret*; *The Holy Spirit*; *A Man Without Equal*; *A Life Without Equal*; *The Coming Revival*; *The Transforming Power of Fasting & Prayer*; *Red Sky in the Morning* (coauthor); *GOD: Discover His Character*; *Living Supernaturally in Christ*; and the booklet *Have You Heard of the Four Spiritual Laws?* (which has an estimated 2.5 billion circulation). He was responsible for developing many partnerships among Christian ministries, more than 800 partner enterprises on the *JESUS* film, for example, to help fulfill the Great Commission.

Bill Bright's wife, Vonette, who assisted him in founding Campus Crusade for Christ, resides in Orlando, Florida. Their two sons, Zac and Brad, and their wives, Terry and Katherine, are also in full-time Christian ministry.

RESOURCES FROM CAMPUS CRUSADE FOR CHRIST

Resources for Evangelism

Witnessing Without Fear
This best-selling Gold Medallion book offers simple hands-on, step-by-step coaching on how to share your faith with confidence. The chapters give specific answers to questions people most often encounter in witnessing, and provide a proven method for sharing your faith.

Reaching Your World Through Witnessing Without Fear
This six-session video provides the resources needed to sensitively share the gospel effectively. Each session begins with a captivating dramatic vignette to help viewers apply the training. Available in individual study and group packages.

Have You Heard of the Four Spiritual Laws?
This booklet is one of the most effective evangelistic tools ever developed. It presents a clear explanation of the gospel of Jesus Christ, which helps you open a conversation easily and share your faith with confidence.

Would You Like to Know God Personally?
Based on the *Four Spiritual Laws*, this booklet uses a friendly, conversational format to present four principles for establishing a personal relationship with God.

Satisfied?
In this new version of Campus Crusade for Christ's popular tract *Have You Made the Wonderful Discovery of the Spirit-filled Life?* you will find a wonderful tool for helping other Christians understand what it means to walk in the power of the Holy Spirit—and enjoy a free, abundant life.

A Great Adventure
Dr. Bill Bright wrote this book as a letter to a business acquaintance who had asked how to become a Christian. Written from one friend to another, *A Great Adventure* explains how you can know God personally and experience peace, joy, meaning and fulfillment in life.

Have You Made the Wonderful Discovery of the Spirit-Filled Life?
This booklet shows how you can discover the reality of the Spirit-filled life and live in moment-by-moment dependence on God.

The Holy Spirit: Key to Supernatural Living
This booklet helps you enter into the Spirit-filled life and explains how you can experience power and victory.

Promises: A Daily Guide to Supernatural Living
These 365 devotionals will help you remain focused on God's great love and faithfulness by reading and meditating on His promises each day. You will find your faith growing as you get to know our God and Savior better.

GOD: Discover His Character
Everything about our lives is determined and influenced by our view of God. Through these pages Dr. Bright will equip you with the biblical truths that will energize your walk with God. So when you're confused, you can experience His truth. When you're frightened, you can know His peace. When you're sad, you can live in His joy.

GOD: Discover His Character Video Series
In these 13 sessions, Dr. Bright's clear teaching is illustrated by fascinating dramas that bring home the truth of God's attributes in everyday life. This video series, with the accompanying leader's guide, is ideal for youth, college and adult Sunday School classes or study groups.

Other Resources

Jesus and the Intellectual
Drawing from the works of notable scholars who affirm
their faith in Jesus Christ, this booklet shows that Christianity
is based on irrefutable historical facts. Good for sharing
with unbelievers and new Christians.

Resources for Christian Growth

Transferable Concepts
This series of time-tested messages teaches the principles of
abundant Christian life and ministry. These back-to-the-basics
resources help Christians grow toward greater spiritual maturity
and fulfillment and live victorious Christian lives. These messages,
available in book format and on video or audiocassette, include:

How You Can Be Sure You Are a Christian
How You Can Experience God's Love and Forgiveness
How You Can Be Filled with the Spirit
How You Can Walk in the Spirit
How You Can Be a Fruitful Witness
How You Can Introduce Others to Christ
How You Can Help Fulfill the Great Commission
How You Can Love by Faith
How You Can Pray with Confidence
How You Can Experience the Adventure of Giving
How You Can Study the Bible Effectively

A Man Without Equal
This book explores the unique birth, life, teachings,
death and resurrection of Jesus Christ and shows how
He continues to change the way we live and think today.
Available in book and video formats.

Life Without Equal
Can Jesus Christ solve the perplexing personal and social problems in the world today? Discover the answer as Dr. Bright explains a dynamic new life in Christ. *Life Without Equal* is a tremendous book for anyone who wants to discover purpose, peace and power for living.

Heaven or Hell: The Ultimate Choice
"Where will I go when I die?" The most important question in life only has two possible answers: heaven or hell. And the choice is ours to make. Get the facts. Eternity is a long time to regret a wrong decision. Good decisions are made with good facts. You can know the facts about heaven or hell— what God Himself says in the Bible.

Written by the Hand of God
Although all of Scripture is inspired by God, only the Ten Commandments were truly written by the hand of God. They were given to us on Mount Sinai as pure principles of godly living. In this practical book, Bill Bright shows how the Old Testament truths about God's standard of holiness are reaffirmed in the New Testament and how the Ten Commandments are relevant to us today.

For these and other resources, visit:

WWW.CAMPUSCRUSADE.COM

Also Available from
Vonette Bright

The heavenly Father does not ask His children to live perfect Christian lives . . . and what a relief, as that is impossible even for the "giants of faith" who have led the Church throughout the centuries! Instead, our God asks us to place our hand in His and walk with Him through the adventure of life. This trust—the kind of trust that refuses to let go of God whether in good times or bad—is at the heart of a life of faith. Vonette Bright, co-founder with her husband, Bill Bright, of Campus Crusade for Christ, has walked with God for more than half a century. In this warm and personal book, she draws on her experiences to share what you can expect on your own faith adventures. You'll explore with Vonette how to take one step at a time with God by living through the power of the Holy Spirit, by serving others and by spreading the gospel, and find for yourself a walk with God—a life of faith—that sustains you, encourages you and gives you hope.

In His Hands
Vonette Bright
ISBN 978.08307.54977
ISBN 08307.54970

Available at Bookstores Everywhere!
Go to **www.regalbooks.com** to learn more about your favorite Regal books and authors. Visit us online today!

Regal
God's Word for Your World™
www.regalbooks.com